Understand Chinese mythology

Teresa Moorey

Acknowledgements

Grateful thanks to Val du Monceau, Chairperson of the Cheltenham Feng Shui society, for much helpful advice and instruction.

Understand
Chinese mythology

Teresa Moorey

Teach Yourself®

Hodder Education

338 Euston Road, London NW1 3BH.

Hodder Education is an Hachette UK company

First published in UK 2001 by Hodder Education

First published in US 2001 by The McGraw-Hill Companies, Inc.

This edition published 2012

Copyright © 2001 Teresa Moore

The moral rights of the author have been asserted

Database right Hodder Education (makers)

The *Teach Yourself* name is a registered trademark of Hachette UK.

British Library Cataloguing in Publication Data: a catalogue record
for this title is available from the British Library.

Library of Congress Catalog Card Number: on file.

10 9 8 7 6 5 4 3 2 1

The publisher has used its best endeavours to ensure that any
website addresses referred to in this book are correct and active at
the time of going to press. However, the publisher and the author
have no responsibility for the websites and can make no guarantee
that a site will remain live or that the content will remain relevant,
decent or appropriate.

The publisher has made every effort to mark as such all words
which it believes to be trademarks. The publisher should also
like to make it clear that the presence of a word in the book,
whether marked or unmarked, in no way affects its legal status as
a trademark.

Every reasonable effort has been made by the publisher to trace the
copyright holders of material in this book. Any errors or omissions
should be notified in writing to the publisher, who will endeavour
to rectify the situation for any reprints and future editions.

Hachette UK's policy is to use papers that are natural, renewable
and recyclable products and made from wood grown in sustainable
forests. The logging and manufacturing processes are expected to
conform to the environmental regulations of the country of origin.

www.hoddereducation.co.uk

Cover image © Orange Tuesday – Fotolia

Typeset by Cenveo Publisher Services.

Printed in Great Britain by CPI Group (UK) Ltd, Croydon, CR0 4YY.

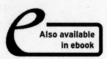

**Also available
in ebook**

Contents

Note on transliteration

Older spelling has been for the most part retained, apart from occasional exceptions, for instance in Yi the Archer (Chapter 3).

Meet the author

Teresa Moorey has written over fifty books on paganism, mythology and related subjects, including the best-selling *Witchcraft, A Beginner's Guide*, and *The Fairy Bible*. One of her books, *Charmed Life* has been featured in *Cosmopolitan* magazine. She regularly does interviews for radio and TV and writes for several magazines including *Woman*, *Chat – it's fate* and *Spirit & Destiny*. She holds an MA in Cultural Astronomy and Astrology and is a Wiccan High Priestess. She is also a counsellor and hypnotherapist. For her entire adult life she has explored the mysterious and the mystical, immersing herself in the mythology of many lands and celebrating the sacred cycles of Nature. Teresa believes that myths have a wonderful ability to change the way we look at things. She also believes that enchantment enriches our experience of life, and that we can all create a little magic through having the right attitude. She has four children aged 14–31 years, and lives in the Cotswolds where she enjoys the beauty of the land and gets inspiration while walking her dog, Paddy.

Introduction

A vital factor in the development of the human race has been its use of symbols to represent ideas or urges that cannot easily be defined. A symbol can magically bring an idea to life by appealing to the creative power of the imagination. It can also offer several layers of meaning in a single image. For example, when Theseus tracks down the Minotaur in the Cretan labyrinth, he lays down a thread to guide his return. This may symbolize divine inspiration, or the link between the conscious mind and the unconscious. The labyrinth itself can be seen as a symbol of the individual's tortuous journey to self-knowledge and of the mysteries of the feminine.

Myths, then, are symbolic stories. They have evolved through oral tradition and they have guided, inspired and psychically nourished humanity for thousands of years.

Myths interpreted

Mythology has been used by poets, playwrights and artists for centuries. The nineteenth century, however, saw the rise of scientific rationalism and of social realism in the arts. Myths were in danger of being demoted to the status of quaint old stories about non-existent gods. A 'myth' began to mean simply a widely held but mistaken belief.

With the rise of psychology, however, myths found a new status – although there was controversy about their origins and functions. Sigmund Freud saw them as expressing repressed impulses commonly found in the personal unconscious. For example, the myth of Oedipus expressed a boy's socially unacceptable desire to kill his father and sleep with his mother.

Claude Levi-Strauss saw myths as stemming from a human need to make sense of the world. By this model, the worldwide myths in which human beings are fashioned from clay by a divine potter, such as the Egyptian Ptah, fulfil our need to know how and why we came to be here. Other widespread myths explain death and the seasons.

Another view focuses on myth as magic. Stories of hero gods descending into the Underworld in the west and emerging in the east reflect the setting and rising of the sun. Myths in which an ageing goddess is reborn as a youthful virgin reflect the return of spring after winter. This kind of myth must have reassured early man. More important, it is likely that the repeated telling of stories symbolizing the rising of the sun, the return of spring or the ripening of crops was a magical way of making these things happen.

Many commentators have noted the similarities between myths in different cultures. One theory is that this can be explained by migration, trade contact and the exchange of myths between conquerors and conquered. There is certainly some truth in this, for example in the interweaving of Aztec and Mayan myths. However, this can hardly explain similarities such as the appearance of 'Trickster' gods: the infant Hermes stealing Apollo's cattle, the Norse Loki cutting off the golden tresses of Thor's wife, Sif, or a similarly mischievous deity of the North American Winnebago Indians.

Jung and the theory of archetypes

The exploration of myths found a new dimension in the work of Carl Jung. Whereas Freud saw the unconscious as being entirely personal, the product of a lifetime's repressed sexual urges, Jung identified a layer of consciousness below this – the collective unconscious. This is a vast psychic pool of energized symbols shared by humanity as a whole. It is filled with 'archetypes': symbolic figures, such as the Trickster just mentioned, the Mother and the Father. They also include the animus and anima, which are the undeveloped and largely unacknowledged opposite sex parts of, respectively, the female and male psyche. Another important archetype is the Shadow, which embodies all that we deny in ourselves and 'project' onto people we dislike. These archetypes form the *dramatis personae* of myth. Thus myths offer a way for cultures to explore their collective impulses and to express them creatively, rather than harmfully.

Myths, dreams and the individual

Jung recognized dreams as doorways between an individual and the collective unconscious. Many dreams, he said, expressed archetypes that might otherwise be projected onto the waking world as irrational fears, delusions or hatreds. Joseph Campbell, who has developed this idea, writes: 'Here we can begin to see a way of working with myths on a personal level, for our own development.' Campbell and other writers have also pointed out that myths are still emerging and developing in the present day. On the social level we see this in the recurrence of mythical archetypes in popular culture, for example in the hugely successful *Star Wars* films.

Jung saw myths as representing the individual's journey towards psychic wholeness. The aim of this book is not only to show the power of myth to entertain and enrich on a narrative level, but also to facilitate this journey. It retells the myths and explores the interpretations – cultural, moral, psychological and spiritual – to which they lend themselves. It also shows how the themes of Chinese myths echo those of other cultures worldwide, in a way that argues a fundamental psychic content common to all humanity.

1

The context of Chinese myths

The mythology of China is as varied and multi-levelled as the country from which it springs. In fact there is no one Chinese mythology. Although there is an undeniable and recognizable quality that is Chinese, China is huge, almost a continent in itself, and contains many different races and cultural groupings. The Chinese mythological heritage does not exactly compare with that of other ancient cultures such as the Egyptians, Greeks, Romans or even the Celts. What is unique about China is its script, a pictographic writing system that cuts across language barriers within China, enabling scholars who would not have been able to understand each other had they spoken together, to communicate in writing and evolve their understanding and concepts. It has also enabled ancient writings to be readily understood, giving rise to a culture that even today, after the Cultural Revolution, has roots and religious practices that extend further back in time than anything in the West. The first empire that unified China, and from which it derives its name, the Ch'in dynasty, came into being two centuries before the Christian epoch, making this a much 'younger' dynasty than that of the Pharaohs, for instance, and coming some 300 years after the birth of Greek Pythagoras. But China, as we conceive it, had existed for many hundreds of years prior to this.

The Chinese have, for many centuries, been a fairly insular nation, for experience taught them that foreigners come to conquer. With the vast Asian landmass to the west, these invasions came inevitably from that quarter, and the Chinese associate the direction of west with death. This is not unusual: being the direction of sunset, many cultures place the homes of the dead, the Isles of the Blessed, in the west. However, to us the west has connotations of peace and rest. In the Chinese system of Feng Shui, the West is the home of the White Tiger and equated with unpredictable ch'i, anger, war, violence and threat. Chinese mythology explores this theme of the cultural 'other', and in the *Classic of the Mountains and the Seas* (see below) foreign lands and foreign people are described as grotesque, barbarous and threatening. This is conveyed in place-names that translate as 'Blacktooth' and 'Threehead', and foreign people such as 'Hairy Folk' and 'Houndarmour'.

The hero of the *Classic* is Yu, whose struggle against the floodwaters is recounted in 'Yu and the Floodwaters' (Chapter 4). The writing of the *Classic* has been attributed to this figure, who appears to be only semi-mythological. The story of Yu includes his slaying of the giant Fang Feng. However, Yu is also credited with killing other troublesome creatures. While this is normal practice for the mythological hero (and in modern parlance such 'giants' symbolize primitive parts of the psyche of which the ego disposes), it is important to remember the especially insular nature of the Chinese approach. This helps us to understand the unique nature of Chinese thought and heritage. The *Classic of the Mountains and Seas* is a major mythological work dating from the third century BCE to the second century CE. In many senses it is a geographical text, reminiscent of the Aboriginal idea of the Songlines, where the terrain comes to life with strange, mythological creatures and events, but it also describes ancient cures for ailments, portents, omens, rituals and similar. The *Classic* illustrates that original mythology emerged in a fragmentary style, and it is reasonable to assume that while this is demonstrably the case with Chinese mythology, it was probably also true for the original Greek myths, before they were homogenized by Homer and others. It conveys the impression of an animist outlook, or a mind-set emerging from animism, where the land itself is considered to be alive. The *Classic* contains many therianthropic creatures, who are both animal and human, and the playful nature of the gods is also demonstrated. This has meaning for us today, for the gods may be seen as embodying forces within us all, and play is a very useful and necessary function, through which we not only learn and grow as children, but also as adults. Play helps us to free parts of ourselves that are otherwise withheld, and may be therapeutic and creative. Myths are part of this 'play'.

Strands of Chinese belief

Politically, China may have been self-contained and sometimes paranoid but from a religious point of view it has been prepared to embrace a succession of faiths and approaches – an attitude that continues in the present day. Tolerance could not always be guaranteed, however, for Taoists were persecuted by Buddhists at times, and vice versa, and this conflict is dramatized in the long tale of 'Monkey King' (Chapter 11).

The original 'religion' in China was that of Wu – shamanism and nature worship. It is probable that this religion was worldwide in earliest times. From this evolved two main strands, one concerning quasi-historical figures and another formed around the world of the afterlife. Such figures as Fu Hsi are part of the first strand, for Fu Hsi taught the fundamentals of civilization, and we meet him in the myth of Yu. The second strand features such personages as the Hsi Wang Mu, Queen Mother of the West, and places such as the Isles of P'eng-lai in the east. In addition we must consider myths in the context of three main faiths, Taoism, Buddhism and Confucianism.

TAOISM

The origins of Taoism lie within the tradition of the shaman, or magical priest. Shamans were believed to be able to travel into the spirit world, for a purpose usually connected with the well-being of the community. This practice was intimately connected with beliefs such as animism (which means everything is alive), pantheism (which means deity is within everything) and polytheism (which means many gods). Although the popular image of Taoism is that of the inscrutable sage, this was a later, more academic manifestation, which intermingled with, and evolved alongside, some distinctly practical applications. In common with pagan religions generally, the material body is valued in certain aspects of Taoism, and a central quest within Taoist practices is the search for immortality – literal, physical immortality. The sense of an interplay between natural law and the abstract laws prevailing in the cosmos, inherent in shamanism, is what gives it its link with Taoism. The Taoists searched for balance within these forces and enshrined the concept that change cannot be forced, only experienced and assimilated. The process of adapting in this way is part of what is meant by following the Taoist Way, immortalized in the *Tao Te Ching* by Lao Tzu (probably compiled in the fourth century). The wisdom and ineffable spirituality of Taoism lends its flavour to many myths.

Figure 1.1 Lao Tzu on his water buffalo on which he was said to have travelled to the West.

Taoism thus has two main components, the philosophical way of Lao Tzu and those like him, and the shamanistic, folk tradition elements. However, Lao Tzu was in fact a contemporary of Confucius during the sixth century BCE, and did not call himself a 'Taoist' for that was a term that evolved over time, and was applied much later. The Taoist Way (which is not exactly a way, or route, but more a state of being) was a state of wisdom that encompassed the totality of Creation. The shamanistic beliefs involved active spirit flight as opposed to the more passive acceptance we associate with Taoism, and had certain things in common with the approach of Lao Tzu. However, Taoism, as we have seen, was also about the pursuit of literal immortality, either by attempting to find the Isles of the Blessed before dying, or by discovering and imbibing an elixir which would confer endless life upon the physical body. The connection between this rather questionable pursuit and the more spiritual aspects of Taoism is rather hard to ascertain, except that following the philosophy of the Taoist Way was reputed to confer immense longevity, and shamanic practices were believed to draw power from a spirit world that exists alongside and intertwines with the everyday world. This spirit world was also a powerhouse on which one could draw, to promote physical health.

Taoism is still extant in modern China, and its practices infuse the daily life of many ordinary families. Many of the stories recounted in the following pages are drawn from this rich and living tradition.

CONFUCIANISM

Confucius is the Latinized name of K'ung Fu-tzu, the honorific name bestowed upon K'ung Ch'iu, meaning 'K'ung the Master Teacher'. He lived in the sixth century BCE in a time of considerable political unrest and feuding between states within China. This was the time leading up to the Warring States Period (480–221 BCE), and K'ung travelled from state to state acting as advisor to the rulers. In what was presumably an effort to avoid what actually ensued, K'ung taught strict order and structure, looking back to a Golden Age in China, when harmony had prevailed. Correct rules for behaviour were laid down. The ruler himself should combine the practical skills of rulership with the wisdom of the sage. In order to pass down this quality through the various layers of government, certain rituals were laid down and K'ung was very strict about these. While such practices may be irritating to read about, in times of insecurity and strife, rigid procedures served an important purpose in maintaining continuity and indeed evoking within the practitioners the mind-set associated with stability. The fact that K'ung's efforts failed did not detract from his appeal, for the episode of the Warring States only served to underline the wisdom of his approach. K'ung's approach is in some respects seen as the opposite of Taoism, in that it does not seek to withdraw and dissociate, but to intervene and manage. However, Lao Tzu, the famous exponent of Taoism, had much in common with K'ung, for the *Tao Te Ching* concerns itself with the management of State. K'ung, however, tried to weld the Tao to a strict set of values, which were able to create virtue by themselves. Correct behaviour is the key, and this is underpinned by a rigid notion of hierarchy, involving strict filial devotion.

Rewards for virtue are believed to come in this life, not necessarily in the Hereafter, as the story 'His Father's Grave' (Chapter 5) illustrates. The Confucian notions of hierarchy are also evident in the bureaucratic pantheon that evolved in China.

BUDDHISM

Buddhism was established in the fifth century BCE by the Enlightened One, the 'Buddha' Siddhartha Gautama. Its teachings were based upon ethics and meditation, and it separated from Hinduism on grounds of ritual, holy writ and social structure. In time a fully Buddhist system of thought developed concerning the transient nature of 'everyday reality' and the necessity of attaining the trance state to achieve knowledge of 'nirvana' or the Ultimate. In the final centuries BCE attempts were made to codify the practices and classify existence, resulting in some quarters in a rationalized and formal approach, while other movements still taught the supremacy of the mystical side. Buddhism was introduced to China in the first century CE and has been adapted by the Chinese to the extent that the mythologies of the indigenous faiths and the imported are intertwined. Early Buddhism consciously created a mythology to give meaning to its practices and beliefs. Even the advent of Buddhism is mythologized in the tale of the Emperor Ming, who had a dream of a golden man flying in front of him as he looked out of his palace. Next day he recounted this to his ministers and was told that in India there was a holy man who could fly and was golden in colour. Hearing this, the Emperor immediately dispatched messengers who went on a long quest and brought back the Buddhist scriptures. Another story tells of one Mu Lien who had achieved nirvana through his efforts over many lives. He now wanted to help his parents, but found that his mother had been reborn as a hungry ghost and even in his status as an *arhat* (a great being or god) he was powerless to help her, because she had committed terrible crimes. Petitioning the Buddha he was told that his mother could be pardoned if all the monks of the ten quarters would come together. Accordingly he invited them all to a banquet on the fifteenth day of the seventh moon, as a result of which his mother was redeemed. Mu Lien then asked the Buddha if all those who were conscious of their filial duty could hold such a festival regularly, and the Buddha granted this request. By such a myth Buddhism reconciled itself with Confucianism. The story of

6

'Monkey King' (Chapter 11) is the most famous example of a story connecting Buddhism with the original religion in China.

The Chinese Pantheon

The variety and scope of Chinese myth and the intertwining of the diverse elements, are reflected in the pantheon. In an attempt to put the myths recounted later in some context, the following is an overview.

Fu Hsi, encountered in the myth of Yu and the Floodwaters (Chapter 4) is, like so many mythical figures, partly historical. In the oldest texts he is part animal. He is a legacy of shamanism, a powerful, magical leader, who teaches humans the civilized arts. Two other beings, Nua Kua and Shen-nung, are grouped with him as the Three August Ones, and some say Nua Kua fashioned humans from the earth. The myth of 'Pangu and the Creation' (Chapter 2) is also a creation myth, that probably imported from Indo-China. These figures parallel, to some extent, the Greek Titans, who preceded the Olympian pantheon.

After the Three August Ones come the Five August Emperors. These were to some extent shamans, but also political rulers. The most famous of the Five is Huang-Ti, the Yellow Emperor, who brought order to existence.

The Taoist pantheon takes shape with the Three Emperors of Heaven: Past, Present and Future. The Emperor of the Present is usually taken to head the government of Heaven, and it was to his celestial presence that earthly emperors made sacrifice. He is also known as the August Personage of Jade, or Jade Emperor, the supreme Yang principle. He is depicted as being married to the Queen Mother of the West, Hsi Wang Mu, the ultimate Yin principle, although she is of extremely ancient derivation and appears in the *Classic of the Mountains and the Seas* as a ferocious goddess. Even in Taoist times she is not precisely benevolent, and comes across as a figure infused with primal power. The Jade Emperor is sometimes confused/merged with the Yellow Emperor, so they appear as essentially the same person. The Jade Emperor, also called *Tiandi*, or 'Sky', had only daughters, for he feared any sons might try to depose him. In this he echoes Saturn/Cronus in Roman/

Greek myth. The heavenly triad has fluctuated down the ages, and is sometimes described as being composed of the First Beginning, or Tao itself at the head, followed by its exponent, Lao Tzu, and beneath him the Jade/Yellow Emperor. As jade is a substance of value found within the earth, and yellow is linked in some systems with the earth, it is fitting that this figure stands at the earthly point of the great triad. However, yellow has special meaning to the Chinese. Before the empire had expanded and combined a number of states, the Chinese nation was, in effect, contained within the bend of the Yellow River. This was the central kingdom around which the attendant states were grouped. China was, and still is, termed the Middle Kingdom, and thus the colour yellow is symbolic of China itself. Besides, Huang-Ti, as spoken, means both Yellow Emperor and Sovereign Ruler, although the pictograph differs. Yellow was thus the imperial colour, and literally surrounded the sovereign.

Beneath the August Emperor is a whole hierarchy of official gods, exactly mirroring their earthly counterparts, so that Chinese

Figure 1.2 The Yellow Emperor's Palace

mythology is interspersed with mention of official documents. Erh-ling is the Jade Emperor's nephew and 'right hand man' replete with magical power and strength, and his doorkeeper, the mighty Wang. Beneath these are ranged a multiplicity of gods, from the Goddess of the Moon (whose story is recounted in 'Yi the Archer', Chapter 3) through to the God of Thunder (who has a blue body), dragon kings who control the rain and watercourses, gods of literature and examinations, gods of happiness, and a multiplicity of gods who take care of mankind, from the hearth to walls and ditches. There is a god of wealth, Ts'ai-shen, gods of the professions and the Eight Immortals. There is also a heavily populated hell that is a combination of Buddhist and Taoist beliefs and comprises possibly the most comprehensive horror story in creation. Hell is a world of its own and is presided over by Yama. It has towns and countryside and provides a full range of grisly, imaginative and enduring punishments for those who do wrong – even fairly minor misdemeanours. But there is also paradise, in the shape of the K'un-lun mountain, presided over by the Queen Mother of the West, and the Isles of the Blessed.

The vast administrative bureaucracy that is the Chinese pantheon reflects the Chinese nation. Like earthly officials, the gods are assessed on a yearly basis. Old gods leave and new ones appear. Many were once mortals, and were 'promoted', and most Chinese gods are, in fact, of human representation. More minor local gods are regularly revered, and these vary from locality to locality.

This forms the background against which the myths are played out. However, each myth stands alone in narrative interest and allegorical meaning. They are just as valid for us today, in the West, although in different ways from our forbears in ancient China.

The literature of China

The very wealth and scope of Chinese literature presents problems for those interested in mythology. Because of the living nature of Chinese myth, many texts are not as old as they claim to be, and material has been selected and subtly altered by various authors in order to support their own beliefs and approaches. The same myth often exists in a variety of forms, and there is no one correct version. It is not possible to make sense of Chinese literature without some familiarity with the principal myths, for they are referred to constantly. In the same way it is not possible to make proper sense of many of the myths without fitting them into their cultural context. In forms of theatre, film, festival, comedy and art, the myths are still a part of Chinese life. In the following pages many myths have been chosen because they are of central importance to the Chinese, or because they tackle a very 'Chinese' concept, such as the Ba Gua, or Pa Kua (Eight Trigrams) which is covered in 'Yu and the Floodwaters' (Chapter 4). These myths also have symbolic meanings applicable to the inner dynamics of people everywhere, demonstrating the universal and powerful language that is myth. The stories represent the vast, diverse and mysterious character of the nation that is China.

Pangu and the Creation

In the beginning there was darkness everywhere, and Chaos ruled. Within the darkness there formed an egg, and inside the egg the giant Pangu came into being. For aeons, safely inside the egg, Pangu slept and grew. When he had grown to gigantic size he stretched his huge limbs and in so doing broke the egg. The lighter parts of the egg floated upwards to form the heavens and the denser parts sank downwards, to become the earth. And so was formed earth and sky, the Yin and the Yang.

Pangu saw what had happened and he was pleased. But he feared that heaven and earth might meld together again, so he placed himself between them, his head holding up the sky and his feet firmly upon the earth. Pangu continued to grow at a rate of ten feet a day for 18,000 years, so increasing the distance between heaven and earth, until they seemed fixed and secure, 30,000 miles apart. Now exhausted, Pangu went back to sleep and never woke up.

Pangu died, and his body went to make the world and all its elements. The wind and clouds were formed from his breath, his voice was thunder and lightning, his eyes became the sun and moon, his arms and his legs became the four directions of the compass and his trunk became the mountains. His flesh turned into the soil and the trees that grow on it, his blood into the rivers that flow and his veins into paths men travel. His body hair became the grass and herbs, and his skin the same, while precious stones and minerals were formed from his bones and teeth. His sweat became the dew and the hair of his head became the stars that trail throughout heaven. As for the parasites on his body, these became the diverse races of humankind. Although Pangu is dead, some say he is still responsible for the weather, which fluctuates according to his moods.

Commentary

Despite the fact that this tale is accepted as a legacy of ancient China, it is probable that is was imported from South-East Asia. However, it is usually ascribed to Ko Hung, Taoist writer of the fourth century CE, who also wrote on the preparation of an elixir of life, and similar subjects. He also wrote *Biographies of Spirits and Immortals*, which is a prime source of mythological material.

THE COSMIC EGG

Myths of a 'cosmic egg' are common to many cultures, signifying the origins of conscious life. In some versions the egg is produced by a mother figure of some description, and even where this is absent, it is present by implication. At one level it merely dramatizes the experience of every individual, starting existence in the egg shape of the womb, which is at first a container and a totality. Conscious, separate existence is achieved when the container is breached, but ends at death, when the constituents of the body return to the earth to become part of the cycle of life. The myth of Pangu on this small level gives meaning to each individual life, and may be a way of processing the idea that the world existed long before we did and will continue long after death. Creation myths embody the internal process of increasing consciousness of the world.

THE CREATION MOTIF

On a larger scale, creation myths are a way for the conscious mind to attempt to explain the infinite and to make sense of a boundless universe. The conscious mind cannot truly conceive of something that has no beginning. However, creation myths of this sort have factors in common with modern scientific theory. The cracking open of the egg itself echoes the theme of the Big Bang, while the shape of the egg connects with Einstein's theory of curved space. According to the Big Bang theory, all matter was at first compressed into an unimaginably dense single point. A reaction took place which caused this to explode and expand into the stars and galaxies. Steve Eddy and Dr Nicholas Campion in *The New Astrology* (Bloomsbury, 1999) write: 'On the physical level [the primal waters] are analogous to the state of the universe immediately after the Big Bang ... composed largely of hydrogen (the H in H_2O, or water) in a vast ocean of unformed potential.'

The myth of Pangu also reflects an animistic view of the world, prevalent in so-called primitive cultures, in which everything is seen as alive, even rocks and soil. It is a vibrant view of creation, and conveys an instinctual respect, a willingness to work with a living earth, rather than an intention to subdue inert matter. Human beings, in the myth, have a quite lowly position. Rather than standing at the centre of the cosmos they are fairly insignificant, taking their place in the natural order. This perspective is echoed in Chinese paintings, where tiny figures are dwarfed by the sweeping vistas of natural features, mountains and waterfalls on varying levels. The development of a spiritual consciousness confers humility and balance.

3

Yi the Archer

Di Jun was god of the eastern sea and the goddess Xi He was his wife.
Together they lived within a giant mulberry tree known as Fu Sang.
This tree grew beyond the eastern horizon, where the sun rises. Di
Jun and Xi He had ten fine sons, who were all suns, and these took
it in turns to ride across the sky, bringing light and life to the lands
below. Xi He was very strict with her sons, and decreed that there
must never be more than one at a time on the daily journey across
the sky, so, while one son made his way over the vault of Heaven, the
other nine remained within the branches of Fu Sang. And so it was
for many, many thousands of years. But not for ever.

The suns grew restless, tired of the same routine. 'Why can we not all
play together, across Heaven?' one of them asked. 'It is so tiresome
waiting here within the branches of the mulberry tree, nine days out
of every ten.' complained another. So one night they decided that
the next morning they would all go forth together. Xi He rose up at
dawn to find all ten of them chasing each other across the sky.

Below, on earth, the people looked up and marvelled. At first it
seemed a wonderful thing that there were now ten glowing suns,
where once there had been only one. However, as day wore on and
the suns chased each other higher and higher up the sky, the people
became horrified. The light given by the ten suns was overwhelming,
so that even within doors, in the darkest corner, no shade was to be
found. The heat seared the ground, rivers turned to vapour and the
crops became ashes. Even the rocks began to melt. From the depths
of the earth, ghastly beasts, woken by the intense light, came forth to
prowl. Di Jun and Xi He saw what was happening and they called to
their sons to return, but they were having far too good a time, so they
frolicked and played while the land burned.

The Emperor Yao heard the cries of his people and saw the plight of the land, and he petitioned the gods for help. Di Jun heard him, and knew that a hero was needed to save the earth. He sent Yi, the archer, with his wife Chang E beside him. Yi had a bow and a quiver containing ten magic arrows. Emperor Yao welcomed Yi, who was eager to get to work on his appointed task. He positioned himself, took out an arrow, notched it, took aim and fired at one of the suns. The sun fell from the sky, with a great explosion, and a black shape hurtled to earth. Dead on the ground there lay a three-legged raven, with an arrow through its heart. Yi again took his bow and let fly another arrow. Again a raven fell to earth, and then another, and another. Yi had warmed to his task. The arrows were notched and winging on their way quicker than the eye could see. Emperor Yao saw what was happening and, coming up to Yi's quiver, he took out one of the remaining arrows, in order that one sun should remain in the sky. With one sun only remaining in the sky, Yi turned to find his quiver empty. And so, on that fateful day, although ten suns had risen in the east, only one set in the west, which is how the world should be.

The people owed a great debt to Yi, who had saved them. Yao thanked them from the bottom of his heart. But Di Jun was sorrowing. 'Alas,' he said, 'nine of my children are dead. Yi, you did as I asked, it is true. But I can no longer bear to look upon you, and be reminded of my dear ones who are dead. You and your wife Chang E must leave Heaven, leave my side forever.'

So Yi and Chang E had to make their home upon the earth, and great was Chang E's disappointment. Yi, for his part, still had many heroic deeds to perform but he was often away from home for reasons which he did not divulge, and his wife felt that he was keeping things from her.

The truth was that Yi wished to return to Heaven, and had been to visit the home of Hsi Wang Mu, the Queen Mother of the West. He had built her a gorgeous palace of the finest jade and fragrant timbers, and this he had accomplished in 16 days. In return she had given him a Pill of Immortality, such as is taken by the gods, so that he might be able to live for ever. The pill was not for one person alone, but had to be shared, and the body needed to be properly prepared and purified before taking it. Yi wrapped the pill in fine silk and concealed it in the roof of his home. While he was out, Chang E noticed a strange glow and she climbed into the rafters to find where it was coming from. There she found the pill, so powerful that it shone through the silken wrapping. She took the package, opened it, and drawn by the magic she put out her tongue to lick it. At this moment Yi strode in, flinging back the door on its hinges, and in surprise Chang E swallowed the magic pill.

The powers of the pill were felt immediately. Chang E began to float. She floated around the ceiling while Yi looked on helplessly, and then she floated right out, through the door that Yi had left open. Nothing that she held could keep her down, so strong was the magic. Crying helplessly she floated higher and higher, up and up, until she came to the moon itself. There she landed, and there she has stayed ever since, with a hare for company. The hare occupies its time pounding herbs in an enormous pestle and mortar.

Yi, left on the ground, was in despair at the loss both of his beloved wife and his chance for immortality. But the gods took pity on him. He built himself a palace on the remaining sun, so that he could be in the sky, near his wife. At full moon, when the moon shines its brightest, Yi is visiting his wife Chang E.

Commentary

Yi is also known as Hou I, an archer who reputedly lived in the time of the emperor K'u in 2436 BCE. Reference to Hsi Wang Mu, the Queen Mother of the West appears in The History of the Chou Dynasty, recorded in the second century BCE, but composed from older material. The legend of Yi, or Hou I, is one of the earlier stories attached to Hsi Wang Mu.

YIN AND YANG

Central to the myth is the theme of Yin and Yang. In the West we are apt to relate the well-known symbol for Yin and Yang to harmony and wisdom. However, the Chinese saw these forces as continually striving, each one struggling for the upper hand, each one rising to its limit, when the other would begin to compensate and to rise in turn, causing continual fluctuation. This concept is central to Chinese thought, which sees the world in a state of continual flux between these two forces – cosmic strife for ever in balance, entropy versus order. This is hardly the picture of universal calm that we in the West have imported, but is probably closer to the truth. In the next story, 'Yu and the Floodwaters', the flood demonstrates an excess of Yin, while Yi and the ten suns shows an excess of Yang. In both myths, the Emperor Yao is the regulating force, although he has a specific task in the myth of Yi, as without his intervention all the suns would have been shot from the sky and the world plunged forever into a state of Yin passivity, cold and darkness. It is interesting that Yi himself, with his energy and his bow and arrows, is a very Yang figure, suggesting that within Yang is the seed of its own destruction, as the black circle appears within the white area (see Figure 3.1). In the following myth 'Yu and the Floodwaters' there appears a similar motif, for it is from the Yin forces (the waves and the darkness of the underground caverns) that the wisdom to overcome them issues. Later in the story of Yi and the Ten Suns, Yi becomes the sun itself, while his wife becomes the moon, suggesting that Yin and Yang are in a state of balance.

Figure 3.1 Yin and Yang symbol

However, it must be noted that the connection of sun/masculine with moon/feminine is not universal, as is often assumed, and some historians believe that the reverse associations were more usual in the majority of early cultures.

FATE AND FEELING

Di Jun, rather than rewarding Yi for obeying his orders, penalizes him for killing his children. This shows the capricious nature of Fate, where obedience and duty are not always rewarded. It also hints at the one-sidedness of Yi, who follows the letter of the law rather than the spirit and who therefore lacks balance. Yi considers only one course of action, the drastic one, of shooting the suns out of the sky, when he could perhaps have captured them without hurting them. Indeed, so great was his zeal, that without the intervention of Emperor Yao he would have shot all ten of the suns. Di Jun's action, in banishing him, underlines the one-sidedness of his approach.

THE CALENDAR

The motif of the ten suns also relates to the formation of the calendar, for at one time in Chinese history there was a ten-day week. The Chinese word for sun is the same as that for day. The seven-day week was not adopted by the Chinese until the fifth or sixth century CE.

THE RAVENS AND THE SHADOW

The ravens that appear when the suns are shot down reveal the true, darker nature of the suns that are at first depicted as carelessly frolicking. The raven is representative of the Shadow. Psychologically, wherever the light of consciousness appears, there must always be a corresponding shadow. In Jungian terms the Shadow consists of the buried or repressed sides of the personality which are usually unpleasant. Projection of the Shadow is a well-known phenomenon, resulting in hatred of persons or things outside oneself, not recognizing that they have acquired this power to enrage and disgust us because of something within ourselves. As a simple example, we may hate untidy people, patting ourselves on the back because we are so orderly, when, in fact, it is our own lack of order in some unrecognized form that we hate and repress. It is an uncomfortable truth that what we hate often tells a tale about us!

The Shadow lies behind racial hatred, and whole cultures have a collective Shadow, such as hatred of whites by blacks (and vice versa) and hatred of the Jews by the Arian race. Thus it can be seen that the Shadow has a most dangerous aspect. Unfortunately, it is all too easy for the Shadow to take on heroic form, for we become self-righteous when stamping out evil. An example of this was the activity of the Holy Inquisition in Europe in respect of so-called 'heretics'. As the emblem of the sun is often related to the hero in myth, it is quite apposite that the destructive suns should be revealed as having black hearts. Here we have an important component of the myth of the ten suns. When Yi shoots them down they are revealed for what they are, the destructive Shadow. But Yi, in his self-righteous zeal, also has a 'Shadow'. In stamping out the destructive suns he is unaware of his own 'shadowy' destructiveness, and for this he is penalized by Di Jun.

The ravens have three legs. At first this renders them more sinister, as deformed creatures. However, the symbolism of the number three is explored in the myth of 'Yu and the Floodwaters' that follows. The ravens, on a practical level, may mean sunspots.

THE PILL OF IMMORTALITY

This reflects the Taoist obsession with immortality. Rather than suggesting spiritual immortality, the Taoists were quite explicitly in search of physical immortality, and many people died of poisoning in the quest for this. At the heart of this may lay the appreciation that by living in harmony with the Tao, matter and spirit cease to be divided and the essential Oneness of all becomes a reality. Nevertheless, many people sought physical continuity. The pill is awarded by the Queen Mother of the West, Hsi Wang Mu, the west being the home or direction of the dead. Hsi Wang Mu was probably a historical figure, but tales about her have been embroidered at great length and obviously have a symbolic basis.

HSI WANG MU AND TRANSFORMATION

The Queen Mother of the West, Hsi Wang Mu, is a very important figure in the mythology of the Chinese and she is especially honoured by women as they approach their fiftieth birthday. This indicates that she is associated with female maturity and passage into the post-menopausal years. She is therefore a goddess of transformation and the cyclical process. She also rides on a white crane. Cranes are symbols of longevity to the Chinese, and believed to be the rulers of ordinary birds, while white is associated with death (see Chapter 4) These birds are also associated with passage, taking immortals on journeys between this world and the next. In the garden of Hsi Wang Mu grow the peaches of immortality, from which she fashions the magic pill in the story. Yi, the hero, labours in service of this goddess in order to obtain transformation. Thus the myth contains several strands of the interweaving of Yin and Yang and the ultimate establishment of natural order, with a single sun and a single moon. Although more subtle than the encounter with the ten suns, the second part of the story continues with efforts by Yi to create balance between Yin and Yang, in the proper establishment of sun and moon. While there was apparently no expressed intent on his part to give immortality to his wife, the pill is always intended for two people, suggesting that Chang E was always destined to become immortal along with her husband.

THE HARE AND THE TRICKSTER

The hare is a prevalent symbol for the trickster, and for transformation. The hare in the moon, pounding herbs, reinforces the theme of the natural cycle and the changes it incorporates. Because of the movements and habits of the hare it has long been seen as a shapeshifter (as the moon, too, alters its shape) and it was also believed that hares changed their gender. The hare represents a stage in the evolution of ego-consciousness, and, collectively, in the emergence of civilized culture this corresponds to the beginning of social behaviour, as we move from the purely instinctual phase into a consciousness of our place in relation to others and the cosmos. In terms of the myth, with Chang E in the moon and Yi in the sun, balance is now established allowing for transformation to a higher level of consciousness.

4

Yu and the Floodwaters

Many years ago, in a time before time, the great Emperor Yao ruled the lands of China, bringing harmony and prosperity. But Yao grew old, and, in the manner of great sovereigns, began to worry about who would succeed him. Although Heaven had blessed him with ten fine sons, none of them seemed fit to carry the responsibility of government. He called before him his chief minister, asking for advice, and the minister told him, 'Your son Chou has a fine brain,' but the Emperor replied that the boy had no true confidence and because of this he liked to pick fights.

The minister then suggested one of the court officials, but the Emperor told him that the man was full of ideas, yet when given responsibility achieved little. One of his tasks had been to cope with the floods that currently plagued the land, and in this he had not succeeded. The Emperor dismissed the minister, to meditate alone and contemplate the endless downpour of the rains.

Learning of the Emperor's distress, the functionaries of the Imperial Court cast about them for help and the name of one K'un was brought to his notice. K'un was grandson of the mighty Yellow Emperor, who had brought order to the elemental chaos at the beginning of creation. K'un had the gift of being able to take the form of a white horse. Nine years he spent creating earthworks and channels to cope with the floods. He watched the people suffer and the very bastions of Heaven under threat, and great was his sorrow. Despite his labours the waters continued to rise, and K'un gave way to exhaustion and despair. Head in hands he sat, while the waters surged round him, and he conceived a dangerous plan.

Within the sacred confines of Heaven there was a magic soil, the Breathing Soil, that if sprinkled upon the waters would swell and grow, so forming enough earth to overcome the flood. Could he steal this? As he contemplated, two strange animals came to him, and advised him on the theft of the magic soil. These were an owl with a horn and a three-legged turtle. To K'un they imparted knowledge of how to conceal his theft and bypass the guardians of Heaven, and K'un did as they advised, keeping the soil within his clothing, close to his chest. But the crime had been noticed and Chu Yung, also called Pray Steam, the god of fire, came after him. K'un ran as fast as the wind, but the fire god flew faster, and at the foot of Feather Mountain Chu Yung slew K'un.

But K'un was no ordinary mortal, to pass unheeded into the Eighteen Hells. For three years his body lay at the foot of the mountain, untouched by corruption and decay. At the end of this time his belly split and from it issued Yu, while K'un himself turned into a yellow bear. Now the Emperor Yao still sought a successor, and finally decided upon one Shun, who was linked by ancestry to Yu and K'un. Shun was an ugly man, having double eyes and a mouth as large as a dragon's. His step-mother with her son and Shun's own father had tried three times to kill him, by fire, burial in a well and drowning in a cesspit. Shun not only survived but remained loyal to his murderous family. Because of his strength and fidelity, Emperor Yao made him his successor.

Meanwhile Yu, in the care of the shamans who had tended his father, was growing to manhood. Like his father he was no ordinary mortal, having the power to change, at will, into the shape of a dragon, or into a bear. He took to himself a wife and began to make a home, but like all the people of China he was menaced by the incessant floods. Shun heard about Yu and, realizing that here was an exceptional man, he sent for him to fight the rising waters. Yu left his home and journeyed to the Emperor's side, where he accepted the commission to combat the floods. Then he journeyed to Heaven where he asked to be allowed to take some of the Breathing Soil. The gods were well pleased with his humility and gave him some of the precious soil. Yu hastened back to earth, seeking out the places where springs came bubbling from the earth and plunging into them in the form of a winged dragon. Against the rushing waters he would fight, pushing on down to where the spring issued, from the underground ocean itself, and there he blocked the source of the spring with the Breathing Soil. Then Yu, the dragon, would return, riding up the spring and out towards Heaven, descending again and again to block the springs, until the only waters that issued were the ones that watered the crops the people were growing.

No more waters came to plague the earth, but still the floods had not dried. Yu sat down beside the banks of the Yellow River and slept, and into his sleep came dreams. He saw himself bathing in the Yellow River, but as the waters came upon him he opened his mouth and drank them dry. Upon the river banks appeared a white fox with nine tails, and so he awoke, staring at the waters, and as he watched, a strange white-faced creature, half fish, half man came towards him, bearing a chart with the Eight Trigrams telling how the river could be quelled. Using these magical instructions Yu began working against the waters, but strange it was that the gods of the lands and rivers did not help Yu. He called them all to a great meeting on the mountain of Kuai Chi, but the giant Fang Feng came late in order to insult Yu. Enraged, Yu beheaded him, whereupon the gods consented to help Yu quell the waters.

In his dragon form, Yu could split rocks with his mighty tail. He formed passes through the mountains and raised great banks to contain the river. Even today you may see Lung Men, the Dragon Gate, and trace the fingerprints of the mighty Yu and his helpers on the slopes of the mountain Hua Shan. While delving at Lung Men, Yu broke out into a cavern in the bowels of the earth, and saw before him in the shadows a menacing shape. He drew close to this creature and saw that it was a divinity with the tail of a serpent, Fu Hsi, the ancestor god. Now Yu knew that the great Fu Hsi had been conceived by his mother through the breath of heaven and carried 12 years in the womb. He brought civilization to humans, teaching them how to cut wood, cook, hunt, make music and choose one mate alone with whom to live. He it was who invented the Eight Trigrams and the Magic Square Lo Shu, where nine digits are arranged so as to add up to 15 in every direction. Humbled, Yu bowed and approached with reverence.

'Lord Fu Hsi, how may I serve you? What brings you here?' Fu Hsi made no answer, so Yu asked again 'Great Lord, the world is troubled, and I labour night and day to stem the waters. Can you help me?'

Again the god remained silent, and so for a third time Yu petitioned him 'O Great One, is it because we have offended Heaven that we are so punished?'

And now, at last, Fu Hsi answered him: 'Yu, the gods have been watching you. Great is your strength, dauntless your endeavours, yet even you cannot succeed alone. Therefore I have come to help you. Come closer to me, Yu, son of K'un.'

Yu drew closer to the god, who produced from the folds of his robe a jade tablet, saying, 'Take this, Yu, son of K'un, and be helped in your quest.' With these words the serpent god vanished. Yu returned to the surface and following the given directions, laboured for a further ten years. Long days and nights he laboured, from the Eastern Mountains to the Western Mountains and from the Mountains in the North to those in the South. Yu's fingers were worn to the bone and his body hair disappeared. He became blackened, twisted and disabled, and his mighty body shrank to half its size, but not until all the waters were vanquished did he allow himself to rest. Then the Emperor Shun looked upon the achievements of Yu and he was greatly pleased.

The wise Shun died and he was buried with respect by his half-brother, so in death some of the wrongs done to him in life were corrected. Yu then ascended to the imperial throne and began the task of counting the population and erecting mountains at each of the four points of the compass. Then he caused the distances between north and south and east and west to be measured and recorded, and was well contented with the harmony of nature when he was informed that the distances matched.

Then Yu received word that a dreadful beast was terrorizing the people. It was in the form of a snake with nine heads and a body so vast that it covered nine peaks, while its vomit was deadly to all life. Yu rode forth to confront the beast, and, spying him, it let flow a copious flood of venom. Taking the form of a dragon, Yu flew above the noxious torrent. The nine heads looked everywhere for him, but did not see him because they did not look upwards. Yu swooped from the sky, and as the wind began to rush about it, only then did the creature realize from whence the attack was coming, but by now it was too late. Yu struck all nine heads from their necks and the creature convulsed in its death-throes amidst the gushing of its own blood.

For a long time it lay dying and the land itself seemed to shrink from it. Three times Yu buried the vile corpse and three times its putrid flesh burst forth to poison the land. Finally Yu interred it beneath a lake, building over it a mound on which he then constructed a tower, and then the beast was at rest. Now Yu caused to be made the Nine Cauldrons upon which were engraved the symbols of the Nine Regions and was thus able to command the loyalty of all. These cauldrons were passed down to Yu's descendants and they possessed the magical quality of being heavy beyond imagination when the True and the Great ruled, becoming feather-light when those that governed succumbed to corruption.

When Yu died the earth had been regulated and the waters brought under control. All was balance, peace and harmony. And so Yu is honoured as the final August Ruler.

Commentary

Yu is referred to in the *Classic of the Mountains and Seas*. The *Classic* is a major source of mythology, dating from the third century BCE to the second CE. It attracted interest when its mythological content was found to be paralleled by a discovery of an executed man within a cave, in about 50 BCE. His mode of execution, the same one as that described in the *Classic*, was meted out to one who had killed a lesser god who was beloved of a greater god. The text survived for a variety of reasons, among which was its value as a geographical treatise.

Yu is recorded as having lived towards the end of the third millennium BCE and as having founded the Hsia dynasty. This was believed to have been a mythical era, but some evidence as to its actuality has been uncovered by archaeologists.

THE THEME OF THE FLOOD
The myth of Yu is built around the theme of a gigantic flood, common to most cultures, as in the example of the biblical Noah, Utnapishtim in the Mesopotamian myth of Gilgamesh and Deucalion

in Greek myth. This theme can be seen as significant on several levels, the first being the literal. For the Chinese it has a special significance because, throughout history, countless people have lived along the banks of two great rivers, the Yellow River and the Yangtze. All the while they were aware that the rivers that gave them life and irrigated their crops could one day destroy their livelihood and their lives. A number of tales illustrate the importance of being able to control flood waters, and the amount of respect due to anyone able to achieve this. K'un and Yu are such people.

On a global scale, it is almost certain that at some time in prehistory large-scale floods did actually occur. Geologists have discovered that gigantic *tsunamis* hundreds of metres in height can be caused by the collapse of a small island, due to volcanic activity. In the present time, such a tsunami would wipe out the eastern seaboard of the United States, for at least 20 km inland. Other, more massive disasters have been postulated, such as collision with a large meteor, such as occurred at the K/T boundary event, wiping out the dinosaurs. Stories of the lost continent of Atlantis may be based on similar fact, with the added possible dimension of an advanced culture that tampered with the environment. At a very basic level, flood myths demonstrate the power of nature and the inability of the ordinary human to do anything about it. These myths are a way of containing the terror produced by this prospect.

Myths of the Flood are also, in a sense, creation myths. Here we have the emergence of life from the 'primordial soup', the formation of Chaos into something meaningful and structured as the waters are channelled and contained. The Koran tells us that from water comes all of life. The foetus grows within the amniotic fluid, and we all begin our existence within this seemingly endless 'sea'. There is no life without water, but water can threaten to swallow what it creates. The theme of the Flood shows the struggle of life to be born. It also epitomizes all births, large and small, from the birth of a human child to the emergence of a creative idea; both have positive and negative aspects, for there is always pain in the effort expended and the act of separation.

At a psychological level the Flood myth relates to the emergence of the ego from the 'sea' of the unconscious and its struggle to rise above it and make sense of it. This was, in all probability, an evolutionary process, as primitive peoples, living at one with the Source, became more aware of their separateness and their ability to think in a detached fashion. Every child growing to adulthood repeats the same process. On a mental level, to maintain sanity the individual must rise above the waters of the unconscious and channel them. Yet the water of the unconscious is still vital to life, as demonstrated in the myth in which inspiration comes from the water itself, in the shape of the white-faced creature. It also signifies rebirth.

SYMBOLISM OF NUMBERS

The number three is repeated several times in the narrative. K'un is, in a sense, the third alternative for the Emperor, for while the Emperor's son and one of his ministers are considered as his successor, this role is somehow combined with the role of flood-fighter, and this falls to K'un. K'un labours for nine years – three times three. One of the creatures that approaches him with the dangerous plan to steal the Breathing Soil is a turtle with three legs. For three years K'un's body lies uncorrupted, before the emergence of Yu, and there are three attempts on the life of Shun (who is linked to Yu, as a relative). The fox that appears to Yu has nine tails, three times three. Fu Hsi has to be asked three times, and the Magic Square he reveals is a product of nine numbers, adding up to $15 - 1+5 = 6$, which is 2×3. The beast described has nine heads, covers nine peaks, and there are nine cauldrons for the nine regions. The beast is only successfully interred at the third attempt.

Three is widely considered to be a lucky number in the West. It is the number of creativity, as in Mother, Father, Child. It is the balance between opposites, such as Yin and Yang which the Chinese saw as being in a state of constant war (rather than complementary and peaceful, as we are apt to assume). Three also signifies the human being, placed between conscious and unconscious, between nature and intellect, mind and matter. Many deities in a variety of pantheons form a trinity. Three relates to our human position as observer of opposites, where this perception of polarities must stand, or there remains nothing but to be reabsorbed into the primal soup, and yet the essential oneness of all is also perceived. There are three dimensions – length, breadth and width – which form the dimensions of the manifest world. In this connection it is interesting that the nine-headed beast looked everywhere apart from upwards, and was defeated because of its lack of awareness of the third dimension. The inability to look upwards may also signify lack of developed consciousness, base instinct unable to rise to self-awareness. The beast is, in some ways, a noxious recurrence of the flood, but this is another stage in the process of development, where the instinctual self becomes vengeful at being repressed. The beast can only be finally quelled by burial in the earth, where it belongs, as the matrix of life.

Ten is another number that features in this myth: Yao has ten sons, but none of them are suitable to rule; Yu labours for ten years before his work is complete. Ten relates to the complete range of available resources, as humans have ten fingers. Where the ten sons are unsuitable, this signifies that current resources are not sufficient. Where Yu labours for ten years and the labours are done, a cycle is successfully completed.

The number 12 also plays a significant role in this myth. Fu Hsi is described as being 12 years in his mother's womb. This relates to the cycle of 12 years, depicted by 12 animals, that compose the Chinese calendar.

THE LIFE OF SHUN

The example Shun displays of filial piety, gives one the impression that the story has been given a Confucian twist, to exalt duty, hierarchy and obedience to one's parents. Yu may also be a 'Confucian' hero, in that he is devoted to duty and organizational skills. Taoist perspective, however, may see the actions of Yu as an interference with natural order, the Way, and the beginnings of humankind's tampering with the forces of nature. It is a tale of the rewards of patience and suffering. It is also a story of superhuman strength, and may have links with the ritual sacrifice of kings, performed in many cultures. In the story Shun faces death by fire, earth and water. This signifies transformation and an experience of initiation, meaning Shun has wisdom far beyond that of an ordinary human, and has passed beyond normal laws, as the shaman was believed to be capable of doing.

THE BREATHING SOIL

This signifies the Air element, the breath of freedom, the ability of the intellect to range far and wide and to remain above the unconscious waters. Because it is, of course, 'soil' we may assume connections with the Earth element, with fertility and constructiveness, that cannot be accomplished while all is engulfed in water. K'un fails in his attempt to gain this soil because he does it by subterfuge. His fate is in some ways reminiscent of that of Prometheus, who stole the fire of the gods in Greek myth, and became a sacrifice for mankind. Yu, on the other hand, employs negotiation and argument, and is thus successful.

YU AND THE DRAGON

Please note that dragons, in their specifically Chinese form, are dealt with more fully in 'Tales of Dragons' (Chapter 12). Yu is sometimes depicted as riding on the dragon, sometimes as changing into it. In Chinese myth, dragons are usually beneficent creatures, and the symbolism here is complex. On the one hand the dragon is the very embodiment of primordial force, the raw power within the earth. In early Chinese mythology, dragons controlled rain and drought, and many Chinese mountains and rivers incorporate the term 'dragon'. However, dragons may also have wings, and as such represent the power to soar, to acquire the broad perspective, to apply intuition. The dragon is a symbol of transformation, linked to the serpent, whose coils symbolize the passage into and out of manifestation. It is significant that Fu Hsi is the serpent god, and that he is encountered underground.

THE FERTILE CORPSE

Yu is born from the corpse of his father. In a sense Yu is K'un reborn, transformed by his experiences. The remains of K'un turn into a bear, possibly signifying that the conscious has separated from the bestial, but also suggesting totemic associations, for K'un is specifically looked after by shamans. Shamans work in close association with power animals in their spirit journeys. The Taoist Chinese were preoccupied with the search for immortality and the *Classic of the Mountains and the Seas* describes 12 deities who are living corpses. Here we have life-in-death which is connected to initiation, and to shamanistic techniques. The bear is an animal linked to the wisdom of the earth. It has the power to discriminate between what is of value and what is not (for example, it instinctively seeks out healing herbs).

HELPFUL ANIMALS

These frequently appear in myths, signifying the often undervalued instinctual qualities, or possibly parts of the personality that function less effectively, but yet need to be taken into account. More specifically, in shamanic traditions animals represent certain powers, and may be very potent indeed as power animals that give protection and guidance in spirit journeys, for these animals are a kind of 'hotline' to specific powers within nature. The animals that appear to K'un are suspect in that they are of no identifiable species, and could be considered deformed. Despite the creative symbolism of the number three, it is inappropriate and unbalanced for a turtle to have three legs, possibly signifying that inspiration was, in this case, coming from the wrong place. The bird with the single horn signifies unity, but again the horn upon the bird is inappropriate. However, these creatures are part of the process that leads to unity and creativity, in that K'un must pass through the stages of the myth before Yu can emerge. These creatures are forerunners of the messengers that come to Yu. The white fox with nine tails, despite the fact it is a mythological beast, is not unbalanced but blessed with its extra, symbolic tails, while the creature, half fish, half man, is in some sense Yu's own alter ego. His father's name, K'un, can be translated as 'Huge Fish'. The fox is white, and the strange creature has a white face. White may be related to the light of consciousness, and also to the feminine, inspiring aspect within a man's psyche, termed the 'anima' by Jung.

THE COLOUR WHITE AND THE FIVE ELEMENTS

Specifically, to the Chinese, white is related to the element Metal. The Chinese have a system of five elements, which symbolize different forms of energy. These elements are Fire, Wood, Water, Metal and Earth. Each person, thing or process is composed of these elements, usually having a preponderance of one of them. Thus a person whose make-up is Fire is likely to be intuitive, compassionate and excitement-seeking, while an Earth personality will be reliable and focused on practical details. Western esoteric systems have only four elements, Earth, Fire, Air and Water, correlating with the four compass points, but the Chinese system is not so very different, for the five elements still relate to these points, with Earth at the centre. The element Metal is linked with the West, and the animal of the West is the White Tiger. Each compass point is related to certain characteristics (which we shall meet again in relation to the Eight Trigrams). The White Tiger of the West is related to the unpredictable, to war, force, strife, strength and danger. For the purposes of interpreting the myth of Yu, we can see that the whiteness of the face of the creature, the white fox, and so on, signalled change and violence. It is not hard to see why the Chinese might relate the West to warfare, because it was from the west that invaders generally came, rather than from the oceans to the east. In many cultures the West was associated with death, and the Summerlands or Isles of the Blessed were believed to be beyond the western ocean. To the Chinese this was also the home of death, and white is related to the occult and to death – it is the colour worn at funerals and the 'people in white garments' are the dead. Albino animals are often considered carriers of the supernatural.

The five elements
The five elements have aspects of Yin and Yang within them, and are part of the picture of Feng Shui (see below and Appendix 1). They have an affinity with the points of the compass – Fire with South, Metal with West, Water with North and Wood with East. This is called The Later Heaven Sequence, arranged by the philosopher King Wen, founder of the Chou dynasty in c.1,000 BCE. The Former Heaven Sequence was believed to have been discovered by the god/ emperor Fu Hsi around 3,000 BCE. The correspondences linked to these Sequences are in the table below.

Symbol name	Compass Later Heaven	Talisman Former Heaven	Element/ Power	Relation/ Family	Number
Ch'ien	N/W	S	Heaven	Father	6
Sun	S/E	S/W	Wind	Eldest Daughter	4
K'an	N	W	Lake	Middle son	1
Ken	N/W	N/W	Mountain	Youngest son	8
Centre	Centre				5
K'un	S/W	N	Earth	Mother	2
Chen	E	N/E	Thunder	Eldest son	3
Li	S	E	Heat	Middle daughter	9
Tui	W	S/E	Sea	Youngest daughter	7

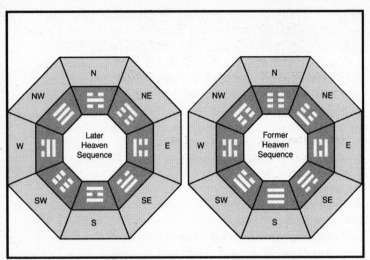

The Later Heaven Sequence   **The Former Heaven Sequence**

Figure 4.1 The Later Heaven and Former Heaven Sequences

In the centre of the circle is the element Earth.

Traits of the five elements

Each element has certain characteristics; can you see aspects of your own personality in these descriptions?

Earth – The Diplomat – The Centre – T'u
If this is you, you are stable and reliable and you believe in moderation in all things. Unless your safety and that of those you care for is compromised your loyalty can be relied upon. You like a quiet life and a peaceful one in the company of friends and family, and you like to help others. You'll attend to the small print but sometimes you dig your heels in over details. You should avoid damp.

Fire – The Magician – South – Huo
Intuition and empathy are your themes and you believe communication is all-important. Hedonistic and sometimes thrill-seeking, you love to be in love. Tedium is anathema to you and you should avoid heat.

Water – The Philosopher – North – Shui

You are on a quest for wisdom and you are imaginative and resourceful. Although you need safety and security in your life, you are independent and can be tough. Intelligent and well-informed, you are truthful, but sometimes you prefer to say little and guard your secrets. You should avoid cold.

Metal – The Catalyst – West – Chin

Order and cleanliness are essential. You like to be in control and to be proved right, and you are precise and particular. Quality is important to you and you are always organized. You should avoid dryness.

Wood – The Pioneer – East – Mu

Often on a mission of some kind, you have a broad vision and a strong purpose, but you are also realistic and practical. Dynamic and always on the go, you can be a tad bossy sometimes and you like to win.

You can determine which elements are important to you by analysing your personality; this will also be revealed through Chinese astrology, the yearly aspect of which is covered in Chapter 15.

THE EIGHT TRIGRAMS

This is a most significant part of the story of Yu, with meanings that are important to modern Chinese practitioners of Feng Shui, and to those who use the I Ching. A 'trigram' is an arrangement of three lines, one above the other, and these lines may be complete or broken. The eight trigrams form the basis of the I Ching (see Appendix 2). Arranged in an octagon they also form the basis of the Ba Gua – a powerful talisman, found not only in Chinese homes but also in Western homes where the art of Feng Shui is employed. The Ba Gua is allied to the Lo Shu, explained in Appendix 1. In the Ba Gua, Feng Shui and the I Ching combine, providing balance and harmony and repelling negative or evil forces. A favourite position for the Ba Gua may be on the front door, especially if the position of the door does not encourage the circulation of chi, or life force.

Thus, in the myth, Yu is endowed with knowledge which comes from the heart of Chinese mysticism, but he is also given practical grounding, for the Ba Gua is related to the compass points. Later in the myth Yu is very careful to establish the four points of the compass, to ensure that all upon earth is balanced and defined.

FENG SHUI

Feng Shui (pronounced 'fong shoy') is the Chinese system of arranging the environment, to produce harmony. It is based on the premise that the way a building is constructed, and the articles positioned within it, can and does have an effect on the subtle energies, and that these can have far-reaching implications for anyone who lives there.

Feng Shui is a cultural narrative rather than a story, bringing a vibrant, mythical life to the environment. While individual myths may be interpreted in terms of the subconscious mind, and its secret dramas, Feng Shui is the ongoing subtle energy fluctuations in a world where reality is not quite what it may seem.

The Five Elements are employed in Feng Shui, both to suit the house to the personality and to draw in certain qualities: for instance, the ideal house faces South, because that draws in light and warmth, while the master bedroom is best placed in the West, encouraging relaxation. For more information about Feng Shui, see Appendix 1.

Only by appreciating the tenets of Feng Shui can we understand how fundamental was the information passed on to Yu by Fu Hsi in the cave.

5

His Father's Grave

Chou had never really known his father, Wen Jung, because he worked in a far-off province. Shortly after he had married his mother, duty had called him away. When Chou was five his father came home for several months, but Chou had been too young then to remember anything much. His father never came back. When Chou was 13 years old, word came that his father had died in far-off Kueichou.

Wen Jung left not only a widow and a son, but elderly parents, too. With his death the money he regularly sent home ceased, and the family were plunged into poverty. Chou's mother did all she could, and the family managed to avoid starvation through her spinning and weaving. But there were few male relatives in the family and so there was no one to journey to Hupeh, where Wen Jung had died, to bring back his body. The family performed all the rituals they could, but without the presence of the body this was not complete, and they worried that Wen Jung's soul might be lost and wandering. Soon the aged parents followed their lost son into the grave. On their deathbeds they begged Chou not to forget his filial duty to retrieve his father's body. Needless to say, this affected Chou greatly, and he felt that a peaceful rest for the spirits of his ancestors could only be obtained through his efforts.

Poverty tightened its cold grip on the little family, but Chou was able to help through his skills as a calligrapher. However, little remained to save to make the long journey to Hupeh. Chou hesitated, and worked harder than ever, but his mind was made up by the tears of his mother as she performed the rites to the ancestors. Whatever the cost he would make his way across the land, to where his father's bones lay, unmarked and without honour. The first stage of his journey was to take him through Beijing.

Leaving all that he had saved with his mother he started for the great city with only the clothes in which he stood. He worked his passage by doing painting and calligraphy. On his arrival in the capital he sought all those who knew of him from his home town, to ask them to use their influence on his behalf, so that he could make the remainder of the journey to Hupeh. Chou earned himself the title 'Chou, the Filial Son' with those who were deeply impressed by his devotion. However, time went by and nothing came to pass. For some unknown reason, despite the fact that official delegations regularly left for Hupeh, Chou was not given a place on one of them. Eventually, he met a Mr Tai, who had known his father, and begged him, on his knees, to lead him to his father's bones. Mr Tai and his colleagues were impressed by the young man's devotion, but Mr Tai warned him, 'The country is dangerous between here and Kueichou, and the city itself is in the grip of strife and rebellion. Your father would be gratified at your filial piety, but your mother needs you, you are young and have no money. Return home, and I will listen out for information about your father's remains.'

At this Chou bowed down and wept, 'I can never, while I live, give up my quest,' he replied. So Mr Tai and his companions all gave him money for the trip he was determined to take, along with a plan for the journey and a letter of introduction in Kueichou. More good luck was in store, for on returning to his lodgings to pack, Chou met another young man who was going in the same direction. He had helpful contacts in local government and suggested they travel together. This worked very well, as it transpired. The next day they set out and worked their way together across the country. But when they had gone half way, Chou's companion detoured to see an old friend, and Chou was overcome with despair and loneliness. Eight days travel away he knew there lived a teacher from his home town, and he decided to visit him for his wise counsel.

Now eight days counted for little compared to the length of Chou's pilgrimage, but Chou was in a weakened state through exhaustion, hunger and exposure to the elements. Halfway to the meeting with the teacher he came to an area where the plague raged and he was overcome by a fever. The innkeeper took the delirious Chou to the temple, not wishing to be saddled with his body. But while there was breath in his body, Chou could not forget his quest. He implored the innkeeper to fetch an official, to whom he explained the purpose of his journey. Drawing from his robes the purse and letter from the men of the town, he asked the official to get him a doctor. It so happened that the doctor knew Mr Chi, the teacher Chou sought, and after weeks of herbal cures he was well enough to complete the journey – but only just. He turned up at Mr Chi's door, rags hanging from his skeletal frame, and was taken in and given a comfortable place to rest.

Mr Chi added his exhortations to all the others who had bidden Chou go back, saying that his mother needed him. But Chou would have none of it, and under the protection of Mr Chi he set himself to earn money by painting. Soon he had enough to resume his journey, setting off through the wildest terrain where fierce animals prowled and the heat and humidity caused his clothes to decay. Bitten by mosquitoes, stalked by tigers and threatened by bandits, Chou clung to his mission. He reached Hankow more dead than alive, as winter set in. Now he worked to gain passage up the Yangtze River, to Kueichou. Nature seemed set against him, but his father appeared in a dream to warn him of hazards in the river, and at last his boat arrived in the vicinity of Kueichou. He saw before him a city deeply scarred by conflict, but in the process of being rebuilt. He soon located the chief of police and showed him the letter from Mr Tai, but although the official was impressed, he was not hopeful. He explained that much of the land had been dug up, graves destroyed and records burned, and that his father had now been dead some 20 years, making the task of finding his body well-nigh impossible.

'In any case, young man, your task is complete,' said the police chief. 'You have arrived at the place of your father's death. Let us go outside the city, where you can take up a clod of soil, bind it in a cloth and pray to the spirit of your father.'

'But I have come so far,' protested Chou, his eyes burning in his weathered face. 'I cannot give up now.'

During the weeks that followed the police chief and his officials searched for records of Wen Jung, but to no avail. Chou was near despair when, by chance, he came upon an old man who had worked for the same official as his father. The old man could remember his father and some details of his illness, death and burial. He even thought he could remember the place where he was buried. Chou was overcome with excitement and rushed off with his news to the chief of police who detailed Captain Hsu to help Chou in the search for his father's bones. They set to work, but the task was hard, the earth rough and overgrown, and it was obvious that while some broken tombstones remained, many had been robbed, or buried. On the third day, as the sun went down, Chou stood exhausted with bleeding hands and made a vow to search for another 14 days for the remains of his father. And on the fifteenth day, if not blessed by success, he pledged to throw himself into the Yangtze rapids at the foot of the city of Kueichou. He raised his eyes and saw the dying rays of the sun were falling on a sunken tombstone, cloaked by weeds. He scrambled to the stone and clawed at the brambles and there, still legible on the weathered surface, was the name of his father.

The warden of the cemetery came to warn him that night was approaching and with it wild beasts were known to arrive. But Chou refused to leave, prostrating himself upon the ground and weeping. He had one more task to undertake, and having come this far there was no way he could be turned aside. Once more the local officials were very impressed, and rallied round to give their help. They came on the ninth day of the ninth month to exhume Chou's father, while the people of the town were celebrating a holiday. Carefully the bones were drawn out, and Chou cut skin from his own arm to seal his father's open mouth. He burned paper money and incense, and lovingly wrapped and labelled each precious bone for the return journey home. For the time being he took the bones back to the temple, while he made plans to go home.

At first it seemed that similar obstacles would delay Chou's return journey as had plagued him on his quest. However, the tale of Chou found its way to the ear of one General Chang who made sure money was made available for Chou to take his father's bones home to his mother. Chou, clad in white for mourning, boarded the boat for Hankow and waved to the throngs of people who had come to bid him farewell. Less than three weeks later he arrived back in his home town, to the joy of his mother, who had waited for him through the long months of his absence.

Now the bones of his father could be laid to rest with the full and correct funeral rites. Chou's ordeal was now over. However, word spread about his devotion, courage and persistence, and he came to be greatly revered. News at length was brought to the Imperial Court, and Chou and his family received honour from the emperor himself. Such are the rewards of the true and dutiful.

Commentary

This myth is Confucian in origin, and is a very thorough example of the filial piety and respect for ancestors that are central to Confucian beliefs. Superficially, this is a story of the rewards of virtue and unselfishness, and as such may seem quite tiresome. The practice of honouring authority and hierarchy is very advantageous for any Establishment. Although some myths may be of fairly recent origin, concocted purely for political purposes, very ancient material has also been used and reconstructed for the same purpose. Bearing this in mind, this myth contains deep meanings that are relevant for us today.

THE ABSENT FATHER

The fact that fathers are very often absent from their families has been identified as a significant factor in the development of children, especially boys. Only an older man can teach a boy what it means to be a man. Where the father is never, or only rarely, present, fantasies can take his place, expectations of oneself, one's capabilities and surroundings which may be unrealistic. Also a sense of identity may be lacking. While the mother is seen as the ground of life – she is present, real and accessible – fatherhood is more mysterious. Father as the source and the seed is not visible, and paternity, before genetic testing, could not be proved. Here there are patriarchal overtones, in that paternity is part of family and social hierarchy, but there are also issues that are vital to the individual. Knowing one's father is part of knowing oneself, at a deep level, and identifying with one's essence and the secret stream of ancestry.

Chou's family, we are told, contains few males. Chou, then, has no male 'input'. Even his grandfather dies while he is young. His father stayed long enough with his mother to father him, and then departed, making a brief appearance when Chou was five. This is a significant age, in that the child is old enough to reflect and differentiate, to some extent, and to recognize his father as an important individual, but he is not old enough to make full use of this, as a role model, to think about what his father means in his life. He is certainly not old enough to fight with him, to disagree, rebel, learn and make peace. Chou's father was not there as Chou became a young man, and there was no one to initiate him into male adulthood. It is significant that he dies when Chou is 13, just reaching puberty. Chou's quest is to find the source of his own identity. It is also a quest for his manhood.

It is interesting that while many helpful males appear in the story, their help is only ever partial. No one takes the young man under his wing. Even the teacher that he seeks out, Mr Chi, offers him limited help. This is a journey that must be made alone. This also applies on a psychological level, and even boys who have a present and helpful father must learn how to be men essentially on their own. Good fathering facilitates this, rather than attempting to turn the child into a clone of the adult. The story is at once a tale of what it is like, inwardly, to have no father, and to have to take the journey to one's own core in order to identify with him, and it is also a tale of what it is like even when one has a present, biological father, for we all have to find our own way to adulthood. Chou makes his way through his own wits, using his talents as an artist, and we may assume that these have been passed down from his father (for we are told only that his mother spins and weaves). While he has been given money, and rather negative advice, it is as he approaches the end of his quest that his father appears to him in a dream, telling him how to avoid the dangers of the rapids. The hardships that Chou encounters are part of his test of initiation, where he finds out what it is like to battle with the elements and be taken to the brink. Thus he discovers his own mettle.

THE MOTHER'S ROLE

It is also worthy of note that several of the male characters tell Chou to remember his duty also to his mother, and to go back to her. But this is a journey essentially away from the maternal. Chou must establish his identity apart from his mother, before he can go back to her, as a man. His mother makes no attempt to stop him – in fact she inspires his quest, to some extent, by her sorrow over the dishonour of his father's corpse. It is often the feminine component of a man's psyche, his inner image of soul and spiritual completeness, that inspires him to develop. In *Families and How to Survive Them* (Methuen, 1987) Skynner and Cleese use the metaphor of a bridge to illustrate how a boy needs to separate from his mother, leaving her side and crossing with his father to the opposite bank. Only when he feels safe and established there is it 'safe' for the boy to come back over, periodically, and to feel close to his mother, or another woman. Without this, the young boy may fear being overwhelmed, and this can affect him in a variety of ways, making him aggressive, or possibly effeminate. In the story there is very little of the 'feminine' at all. We might interpret the wild terrain as symbolizing the negative aspects of mother/feminine which have to be overcome (the land as soil of origin, wild beasts as the 'devouring mother' who will not allow separate existence to her offspring). Once Chou's purpose is accomplished, all obstacles disappear and his journey home is smooth and speedy. When Chou returns to his mother he has established his separation. He is no longer just a skivvy but a bringer of honour and fortune of the highest kind.

THE WILDERNESS

The wilderness through which Chou struggles is also a metaphor for the wilds and chaos of the unconscious and Chou, as a hero figure, personifies the conscious personality that needs to encounter this for creative inspiration. Chou meets the challenges and dangers and brings back knowledge of his own essence (the bones of his father) which he can 'earth' in his personality, as he buries the bones of his father in his native soil.

NUMBER SYMBOLISM

The ninth day of the ninth moon is specified as the day when Chou exhumes his father and claims the bones. The creative meanings of three, and three times three, are examined under 'Yu and the Floodwaters' (Chapter 4). There is an element of the sacred here, which may relate also to the Triple Goddess – maiden, mother and crone. Goddesses are also often found in groupings of nine. The Triple Goddess relates to moon phases, waxing, full and waning, and there is a reference to the 'ninth moon'. Chou is 13 when his father dies, and there are 13 lunar cycles to one solar cycle. Chou promises himself that he will search the ruined graveyard for 14 days, and kill himself on the fifteenth, thus pledging his efforts for half a lunar cycle. These factors indicate that what is happening with Chou is a cyclical process, and the moon presides over the cycle. It also may indicate that Chou's journey receives the unseen blessings of the feminine.

The King of the Underworld

The Chinese spirit world is exactly like the material world. There are systems, courts, forms to fill out and official procedures to follow. In the Underworld there is a series of courts to judge dead people, to decide upon punishment and to settle upon the next life to which the individual will be sent. Souls are weighed, and if found to be heavy, they are passed to the next court to be judged. The nature of the court is determined by the crimes of which the soul is guilty. These include theft, murder, and other major offences, but also more minor things such as lying and lack of filial piety. Ghastly punishments await the guilty, from being fed to wild beasts, to being burned in flames and other horrid and inventive tortures. Each court sends the condemned to a different section of hell. Having passed through all of this, each soul reaches the tenth court, which is the final one, and here a decision is made regarding the next life the soul will have upon earth. Souls who had been good do not have to pass through the hells but go straight to the Wheel of Transmigration, where they are redirected into new lives as members of the aristocracy, while those who are evil are sentenced to lives of poverty and hardship, or even as animals. However, they have the opportunity to improve themselves, with effort, and so earn a better life the next time around.

In China, long ago, there was a Buddhist monk called Ti Tsang Wang who did not sleep like other people. Instead, when night fell and the moon rose, he sat erect in a coffin, never surrendering to the sweetness of sleep, or the comfort of a soft bed. As the years went by and his lack of sleep seemed to make no difference to his health, people began to believe there was something very special about the man. At the grand old age of 99, the monk died, and was prepared for burial in the very coffin in which he had spent all the nights of his adult life. For the first time he lay down, and seemed indeed to be peacefully asleep. But even in death he was different for his body did not decay. Unlike ordinary folk, who leave their bodies and journey to the Underworld as spirits for their souls to be judged, this monk went in his mortal body.

The monk passed by the courts and the different hells and stood by the Wheel of Transmigration. The soul of a woman called out to him and he recognized a neighbour of his mother's. She cried that she knew him, and that he must know that his mother's soul was still in hell, suffering unspeakable torture. The monk was distraught, for he had assumed that his mother had been reborn into a pleasant life. He hastened after the neighbour's soul, but she was being offered the potion of forgetfulness, that wipes out all memory both of past lives and of the punishments of hell. Ti Tsang Wang was too late, for she had drunk deeply and could remember nothing.

Now there was nothing for Ti Tsang Wang but to return to the hells he had avoided and approach the throngs of officials that administer each of them. Each of these has his own task, to record punishments administered, their duration, and the sins giving rise to them. The monk was sure that his mother's life had been very good, for she was a kind and caring person of whom everyone spoke well. Each official insisted that procedures must take their course, and Ti Tsang Wang didn't know where to go to press his claims. However, he was no weak ghost drifting through the hells, he still had his body and so was a force to be reckoned with. Despite repeated official denials and the assertion that there could be no exceptions to the laws of the Underworld, he insisted that his mother was innocent, and that the judgement could not apply to her. He went from court to court, jailer to jailer, seeking news of his mother and all the while screams and cries surrounded him from the souls being tortured. This tore at the heart of Ti Tsang Wang, who knew that as his mother had cared for him in life, so it was his duty to look after her, where he could.

Achieving no success, and with the slamming doors of the many gaols ringing in his ears, the devout monk could think of only one thing to do. He would hold a banquet for all the souls of the monks that were in the Underworld, before they passed to the Wheel of Rebirth. It was not difficult for him to arrange. He had been famous in the religious community during his life because of his way of spending the night upright in a coffin, and all the deceased holy men flocked to his table. There they made lots of noise and caused a great disturbance. This was too much for the officials, who simply couldn't manage to do their work and to keep the necessary order with all this noise and merry-making going on. The authorities gave up. Some say the Buddha himself interceded. At all events, agreement was reached to release the soul of his mother before the allotted time, although she was only given the body of a dog. Now the monk had succeeded, and it was time to follow his own destiny.

Ti Tsang Wang assumed that now he would be passed to the Wheel of Rebirth to go back to earth as a superior being, for he had passed to the Underworld with his body intact and managed to get his own way. But the ways of the gods are inscrutable and there was another role selected for the persistent monk. Because he had been so effectual in the places of the dead, it was decreed that he should stay there. Now he was officially given his name, Ti Tsang Wang, which means 'King of the Earth's Womb', and he took his place as Lord of the Underworld. He now reigned supreme, even over Yama, judge of the dead, and he had two demons at his side for jailers, one with the head of an ox, the other with the head of a horse.

Commentary

This myth was alluded to, in a slightly different version, in Chapter 1. The origin of the myth is confused, but it is based on the life of one Chin Ch'iao-chio, a monk of noble lineage, from Korea. He came to China during the T'ang dynasty in the eighth century CE, and established a ministry on the banks of the Yangtze. It is a Buddhist myth with Confucian undertones and reconciles the two faiths. The Chinese model for hell developed with the advent of Buddhism into a complex system including 18 different hells attached to ten judicial courts.

THE UNDERWORLD

The Chinese Underworld is as fearful as that of any culture, and considerably more so than some. Possibly this is an instinctive attempt to balance the cerebral and idealistic elements within the culture, where a high standard is generally expected of gods and humans. In general the Underworld represents the collective unconscious as well as the individual. It is where the cultural remnants of the past settle and linger, and is the repository for the individual in terms of his or her unlived life and potential. It is that within us which never sees the light of day, and this is often distorted, feared, repressed, and misunderstood. Rivers of Forgetfulness are a common feature and, in the case of the Chinese, the equivalent is a Potion of Forgetfulness, imbibed by the soul as it comes out of the Underworld (although the Chinese believe that the soul still recollects the pain for purposes of learning). Rivers or Potions of Forgetfulness are therefore characteristic of the nature of the unconscious, in that we are oblivious to it. The River of Forgetfulness is also the mirror-image, or antithesis, of the waters of life.

THE HERO IN THE UNDERWORLD

Myths of many cultures abound with tales of the hero who goes down into the Underworld and emerges at length victorious, carrying off some prize, although usually at a price. This is symbolic of the journey of the ego, or conscious part of us, that must at some point brave the terrors of the unconscious, in order to grow in strength and become enriched. It is part of the journey of life that we all undertake, as we emerge from childhood and become conscious that all is not as simple and manageable as we thought.

The journey is never easy, and we may have to encounter guardians who are threatening or obstructive. In our story, these are the many jailers and judges who, with bureaucratic intractability, refuse even to consider the request of the monk. These 'obstructions' often represent the 'inferior' parts of the personality, which do not function smoothly. In a person of a very logical disposition, for instance, this might be the feelings, which tend to confuse. For a 'feeling type' intellect may be a trap which interferes with smooth passage, for the very practical the imaginative realm may pose a threat, and for the inspirational person, the material world may pose a challenge. However, in our journey through life it is important that we learn to work with all aspects of our humanity, and indeed at life's crises, when we are plunged into our private 'hell', it is these parts that we have to confront. In a similar way the monk confronted the officials of hell (note the Kafka-esque nature of the Chinese hell, where bureaucracy bars the way!). Anything that bars passage into or through hell mirrors the very real difficulties of the ego in 'getting down to it'.

The losses that we face in life presage the final loss, which is death itself. As we experience these losses we may become depressed, and face a kind of 'death' as we enter our Underworld. Myths such as this are a way of processing such passages. The descent to the Underworld is a journey of recovery and of finding inner resources, whatever the difficulty.

However, our hero in this story, the monk, does not emerge victorious from the Underworld, but remains there, albeit as a very powerful figure. We can interpret this as arising from the sheer outrage of his demands, which show no respect for the domain of hell. He is guilty of hubris, of challenging the gods, and while he is rewarded in part by the release of his mother, his fate is to stay. In psychological terms this is because the balance has not been reached between conscious and unconscious minds. The ego wants to seize all that is valuable from the nether regions, without due respect or sacrifice. The monk does not even die to go down there; therefore he makes no transition, no passage. His fate symbolizes being trapped in the unconscious or gripped by some unconscious dynamic that cannot be brought to the surface and redeemed. So the victorious monk becomes King of the Dead, presiding over a dead world, and all the horrors that he had sought to bypass. However, his true title, 'King of the Earth's Womb', hints at the potentially creative nature of the place.

LIVING DEATH

It is those who do not recognize the existence of the unconscious mind who are most likely to fall victim to it and to be in some way trapped. It is interesting that the monk, during his lifetime, never lay down to sleep. He sat in a coffin, the vehicle of eternal rest, wide awake. All the while he insisted on not surrendering to the unconsciousness of sleep he was, in fact, in a kind of living death, where he had no connection to the deeper wells of his being. Thus his 'reward' is to be stuck within the unconscious/hell, and never to be reborn into the land of the living. This is a metaphor for all those who will not 'go down' and surrender to what lies within, which may show itself in daily life as depression, loss and mourning. It is only through such times that we can be transformed and reborn.

HELLFIRE

Fire is an image that pervades many concepts of hell. It is a transformative element. In particular it may signify the sacrifice that all life makes for the continuance of the cycle. While death is naturally a subject of dread, when seen from a wider perspective, it is evident that life cannot be perpetuated without death. But to the ego this is horrific, hence the imagery of fire.

THE ANIMAL HEADS

The demon jailers with the heads of an ox and a horse may signify the instinctual and less differentiated parts of the personality that remain in the 'underworld' of the unconscious. Both animals are powerful, and the horse is also an animal of passage, often associated with the Underworld or spirit world. The fact that the jailers do not have human heads, but only human bodies, reinforces the fact that they do not have the power of rational thought.

THE ABSENCE OF THE FEMININE

The description of hell contains nothing feminine, apart from the woman who knew the monk's mother, and she soon drinks the potion and forgets. Even the mother herself never actually appears in the story, but we understand that she is reborn as a dog. This suggests that the anima, which is the inner feminine part of the monk, is lacking. The monk's mother may represent his anima, but he does not properly regain her, and she becomes an animal, rather than a spiritual force.

THE EMPTY KING

This myth, which on the surface seems to be an exemplary tale of filial piety, courage and persistence, and which seems a kind of Confucian and Buddhist 'morality tale', has a wealth of hidden meaning. The empty status of the 'King of the Earth's Womb' is underlined by the Chinese celebration, for he is worshipped on the thirtieth day of the seventh moon. Chinese months vary in length, so if the month has only 29 days, no ceremony is conducted.

7

The Eight Immortals

The Eight Immortals are not precisely gods but legendary figures who achieved immortality through following the Taoist Way. They are welcomed at the table of the Jade Emperor. They are a motley crew and continue to form inspiration for Chinese art and drama. They did not appear in folklore until the thirteenth or fourteenth century, but their attached legends put them in a much more ancient context. The Eight Immortals represent all aspects of humanity: youth, age, male, female, rich and poor. It is hard to see how they came to be linked together. However, at least three of the characters are historical people, and they all live on the Isles of P'eng-lai, the eastern paradise. The following are the Eight Immortals, in the traditional order according to seniority, together with some of the surrounding myths.

HAN CHUNG-LI

The name 'Han' is said to have come from the Han dynasty in the first century BCE, when Han Chung-li lived. He is a mature man with a rounded belly and careless manner. One of his biographies describes him as an officer at court, who became a nobleman with the post of Marshal of the Empire, but who, in his old age, became a hermit. He had the power to make silver from other metals and materials, and would give the wealth so generated to the poor.

One day, as he sat in his dark cave, contemplating the Way, there was a strange rumbling from beneath the earth. Chung-li watched, as great cracks snaked through the stone walls around him. Motionless and serene, he awaited his fate. The cracks grew wider until the walls split apart, but the mountain did not fall upon the hermit. Instead a new chamber revealed itself, from which issued a strange light.

Chung-li arose and went to investigate. He found there a casket, fashioned in finest jade. It opened to his touch and revealed to him the secrets of immortality. Being the sage he was, he understood these secrets and was able to follow the instructions therein. When this was completed, the cave was filled with unearthly music and vapours in all the colours of the rainbow, and a magical stork flew in. Upon the back of this bird he flew to the Isles of P'eng-lai. When the T'ang dynasty ended in the tenth century, he passed on his secrets to the third of the Eight Immortals, Lu Tung-pin, whose story follows. He is known as the True Active Principle, and he represents people in the military. He has two emblems, the Peach of Immortality and a fan made of feathers.

CHANG-KUO LAO

The second of the Eight Immortals is also regarded as a historical figure, from the seventh and eighth centuries. He represents the old, being himself an old man, and he brings the gift of fertility to young couples.

Chang-kuo Lao was repeatedly invited to come to court, but when the Empress Wu finally prevailed upon him to come, he fell down dead at the temple gate. There his poor body lay, decaying and eaten by the worms. However, miraculously, he revived, his body reshaped itself and he acquired greater magical powers. He journeyed to the court, where he was welcomed by Emperor Ming Huang. All were impressed by his abilities, for he could turn birds to stone by pointing his finger at them, could drink poison as if it were wine and could become invisible at will. When he was over 100 years old, the Emperor Hsuan Tsung asked Fa-shan, a Taoist sage, about Chang-kuo. Fa-shan replied that if he dared speak about him he would drop dead, and only Chang-kuo himself would be able to revive him. Accordingly, the Emperor promised that he would ask Chang-kuo's forgiveness, if this happened. Fa-shan then whispered to him that Chang-kuo was really a white bat, and then fell to the ground before him, lifeless. The Emperor summoned Chang-kuo and humbly asked for his forgiveness, whereupon Chang-kuo sprinkled water on the white face of Fa-shan, bringing him back to life. Soon after this Chang-kuo fell ill and went back to his mountain hermitage, where he died and was buried by his followers. Later, his tomb was opened up, but there was no sign of Chang-kuo's body inside it.

Chang-kuo had a magical white donkey, on which he travelled everywhere, often over thousands of leagues in a day, and pictures show him sitting on the donkey, facing its tail. When at rest the donkey could be folded, like a piece of paper, but it regained its shape when the master blew water upon it. Chang-kuo carries a peacock feather or one of the Peaches of Immortality, and a paper horse is his emblem.

LU TUNG-PIN

He is regarded as a real, historical figure who lived in the eighth century and is believed to be author of a treatise on morality, the Kung Kuo Ko. In some orders, he is listed as the last of the Eight Immortals, and around him cluster the greatest number of stories. The tale of his meeting with Chung-li is the most famous, and is known as 'The Rice Wine Dream'.

Chung-li stayed in the Imperial City, Chang-An, amid the bustle of entertainment, official banquets and petty intrigue. Wishing to detach from all of this, he left the court, meaning to walk until he had found a place of peace. Outside the walls of the city he stopped to rest at an inn commonly frequented by travelling officials. Later that day along came Lu Tung-pin, preoccupied by his work and his ambitions, for in those days he was no immortal but a man of high rank in government, who wished to increase his power and status to the further glory of his family. The aged immortal sat sipping his rice wine and looking upon this important personage who had arrived. He saw that Lu Tung-pin was not merely an official and a scholar, but also a man who studied philosophy and reflected deeply. He invited the younger man to drink wine with him, and as the bright day dimmed into dusk, the two sat, discussing the Tao. Many questions filled his head, but Lu Tung-pin found that he was overcome by the wine. While the servants cleared the tables and the firelight dimmed, his head sank onto his chest and he slept.

While he slept he had a long and vivid dream. He obtained the favour of the Emperor and was given high responsibility, which he wisely discharged. Promoted to a post within the court, he became respected, even feared, by all. He took part in decisions taken at the highest levels, and honours were showered upon him and his family. But, in the way of powerful people, he made many enemies and aroused much envy. Even the Emperor came to resent him, and eventually dismissed him. His enemies saw their chance and closed in, telling the Emperor many false tales of his conniving and dishonesty. Lu Tung-pin was exiled, his family executed and the ancestral home stripped of its assets and left to rot. Alone and penniless, Lu Tung-pin wandered from village to village, unknown and mourning. One night he found an inn and took rice wine, sitting alone and weeping until he fell asleep. Then he awoke, at the inn, with Chung-li beside him, smiling gently.

Lu Tung-pin took himself to his bed, but he did not sleep. The next day he sent his servants away and cancelled his engagements in the city. Alone, on horseback, he followed the sage. In his heart he now knew that the true Way had nothing to do with worldly gifts and status. They went together into the mountains, where Lu Tung-pin studied with the master for many a long year, until he too became an immortal.

Lu Tung-pin would travel as a seller of oil, and he gave immortality to anyone who did not ask for more. Only one old woman was satisfied with what he gave, and he threw magical rice into the depths of her well. From that day onwards the well yielded only wine and the old woman grew very wealthy.

Lu Tung-pin was a skilled swordsman and carried a magic sword that made him invisible. With this he travelled the land, vanquishing evil and doing good. He is depicted with his sword and sometimes with a fly-whisk, symbolizing the fact that he too could fly. He is also shown holding a male child, bringing the promise that descendants will be members of the ruling classes. He has been given the title Pure Active Principle and he represents students.

TS'AO KUO-CHIU

Ts'ao Kuo-chiu was the brother of the Empress Ts'ao, and lived in the eleventh century. His symbol is a court writing tablet and he is representative of the nobility.

One day a scholar was travelling in the company of his young wife. The Empress's younger brother, Ching-chih, saw that the young woman was very beautiful, and invited the couple to his apartments in the palace. There they were seated on couches of satin and offered the finest wines and meats. The scholar grew mellow and relaxed, and as he sank back upon the soft cushions the brother of the Empress came towards him and slew him. His wife shrieked and tried to revive him, but Ching-chih seized her and tried to rape her. When she fought him off, he had her thrown into the dungeons. But the spirit of the scholar appeared to Pao Lao-yeh, who was Imperial Censor, and wailed for vengeance to be taken on the evil prince.

Meanwhile, Ts'ao Kuo-chiu advised his younger brother to order the execution of the hapless young woman, and so Ching-chih ordered that she be thrown down a well. The spirit of the planet Venus rescued her, and she was then able to escape the city, but on her way she spotted a procession and thinking it was that of the Imperial Censor Pao Lao-yeh she went up to the carriage to tell her troubles. But within the carriage was Ts'ao Kuo-chiu, who cried to his attendants that this woman was being disrespectful to him. He had her beaten with poles of iron until she appeared dead.

Fate, however, was on the side of justice. Miraculously the woman revived and went in search of Pao Lao-yeh, who was incensed. Both the brothers were immediately arrested and the younger one executed for murder, despite the protestations of his father, the Emperor. Speedily, the Emperor declared an amnesty for all prisoners, and Ts'ao Kuo-chiu was released. Realizing that his life had been vain and meaningless, Ts'ao gave up his status and took on the life of a hermit.

LI T'IEH-KUAI

'Li With the Iron Crutch' was taught the knowledge of the Way by Lao Tzu himself. His studies almost done, he was called to Heaven, but before leaving he instructed his own disciple, Lang Ling, to watch carefully over his body, and to arrange to have it burned if he did not revive after seven days. Lang Ling watched faithfully by the inert body of his master, leaving his side only to get water and enough food to keep him alive. But on the sixth day word arrived that his mother lay dying and was calling for him. Lang Ling did not know what to do. He could not leave the precious body of his master without proper attendance or submit him to the dishonour of not being buried without due attention.

Less than a day was left before the allotted time-span would be complete, and Lang reasoned that by now it was most unlikely that his master would come back. Sorrowing for his master, and for his mother, Lang burned Li's body and set off with all speed. But Li returned from Heaven, to find only ashes where his own body had been, and the only home that was left for his spirit was the body of a beggar, lying nearby. The beggar had died of starvation, his body was twisted and lame, and his hair matted. He wanted to change the body, but Lao Tzu advised him to keep it, bestowing upon it a gold headband, a life-giving gourd and an iron crutch for support. Following his servant to the house of his mother in the guise of the beggar, he found the poor boy prostrate with grief beside her lifeless body. He poured liquid from the gourd into her mouth and revived her.

Li's symbols are the iron crutch and the life-preserving gourd. He represents those who are sick, and he is depicted on signs outside the door of pharmacists.

HAN HSIANG-TZU

Han Yu was a great philosopher and poet of the T'ang dynasty in the eighth and ninth centuries. He taught that there are three elements in human nature, the good, the evil and the balanced. Han Yu protested to the Emperor about the extreme reverence being paid to Buddhist relics and was subsequently banished to Canton, which was then a wild and savage terrain. However, Han Yu earned the reverence of the local people after he vanquished a huge reptile that plagued them.

Han Hsiang-tzu was the pupil of Han Yu, and although he soon outstripped him in wisdom and ability, he accompanied him into exile, correctly prophesying his return to prominence. Han Hsiang-tzu was also taught by Lu Tung-pin, and he obtained immortality by being dropped from the top of the Immortalizing Peach Tree. A flower basket is his symbol and he represents the cultured section of society.

LAN TS'AI-HO

Of the Eight Immortals, Lan is the most foolish, for all his behaviour is inappropriate. For example, when the winter snows lay on the ground Lan made his bed in them, and when the summer sun blazed he wore thermal undergarments. He was a beggar, who wandered around wearing only one shoe, a belt of wood strung around the middle of his torn blue garments. He would sing, beating time with his stick. He threw money on the ground for the poor. Lan was, seemingly, either impotent, homosexual or a female in disguise. Little is known of his origins, but his passage into immortality is recounted. Once, at an inn, he drank so much that he blacked out, and was seemingly rewarded by being carried away on a cloud, leaving his single shoe and old blue robe behind him. A lute is his symbol, and socially he represents the poor.

HO HSIEN-KU

Ho Hsien-ku was reputedly born in the eighth century, with six hairs on her head, after which no more ever grew. A young woman, she is sometimes depicted as playing on a reed mouth organ, given to her by Lu Tung-pin. She also holds a magic lotus and is depicted with a full head of hair, despite the myth.

She also had the gift of 'dreaming true' and of receiving messages in her dreams. One night she dreamed she was being shown the way to immortality. She was to go to the Mother of Pearl mountains, which rose near her dwelling, and grind up one of the semi-precious stones that lay there in abundance. When she awoke she went immediately to the mountains, to do as she had been bidden, and accordingly she became immortal. After this she simply spent her time drifting happily around the mountains, plucking wild berries which she brought home to her mother. Hearing of her special abilities, the Empress summoned her to court, but on the way there she disappeared – though she was reported as reappearing in several different places later on. She is the representative of single women and her symbol is the lotus.

Commentary

The Eight Immortals are the most popular group of deities in the mythology of China. There is a historical basis for some of the figures, although they could never have encountered each other as mortals. It is unclear why this grouping was actually made, and historically it dates back no further than the Yuan or Mongol dynasty, 1260–1368 CE. However, there are many legends that have been created about them, placing them in very ancient settings

In common with many myths of a Taoist origin, the preoccupation with immortality is evident. Immortality, it seems, is literally available and is not merely won by wisdom and study, but can be gained through knowing what to ingest. Beliefs such as this may help to cope with the reality of a harsh world, but are also an allegory for the eternal life of the spirit. The fact that they are eight in number conveys a sense of balance and groundedness, for there are also eight directions in the compass. Thus everlasting life is firmly pegged down within the here-and-now.

LIFE PASSAGES

The first and the last of the Eight Immortals both display an affinity with instinctual wisdom that resides within the natural world. Chung-li receives revelation when the walls of his cave split apart, and Ho Hsien-ku obtains immortality through ingesting stones. However, the material world can also be transcended, for several of the immortals have transformative qualities. Chung-li can change the nature of metals, like an alchemist. Alchemy involves the separation of the various components of life, and the realization of the true relationship between them. It is concerned with the search for the true meaning of life.

Chang-kuo Lao has magical powers, for he can shape-shift and rise from the dead. He is 'really a white bat'. White was the colour of death to the Chinese and the bat is a creature of darkness. Even to speak of this, as Fa-shan demonstrates, evoked death because the mention of Chang's name acted like a spell. This contains echoes of older, shamanic traditions, from which Taoism was born. It also reflects the internal processes of growth within the human psyche, whereby the unconscious mind influences development, so that what is unconscious may become conscious. It contains the understanding that life and death are part of the same process, and that the only constant is change.

This is reinforced by the interesting fact that Chang, the 'white bat' who has died and come back to life, is also the bringer of fertility. The myth of Chang, at an unspoken level, conveys the idea that all of life's passages are, in a sense, one, and are not to be feared, for Chang has mastered them. His donkey that is restored to life when he blows water on it is another example of his power over life, for water is the source and the home of life, and Chang's breath conveys it. His method of travel, going one way while facing another, shows that he exists both in the past and the future, having awareness of both dimensions.

DETACHMENT

The story of Lu Tung-pin and the rice wine dream is perhaps the most graphic. It states clearly that life is a dream, and to progress spiritually it is necessary to detach from it. This is reinforced by the fact that Lu rewards the old woman who was satisfied with her measure of oil. However, she was not given blessings for being unselfish and undemanding, but because she had the wisdom not to be over-ambitious. This accords with what Lu Tung-pin himself discovered in his dream – that too great an ambition is futile because there is no way to make secure what one has attained. Lu Tung-pin with his sword is strongly linked to the rational mind that 'cuts through' what is irrelevant and misleading with the sharpness of intellect.

AMBIVALENCE

The myth of Ts'ao Kuo-chiu illustrates the value of ambivalence – that there are often two sides to things and that right and wrong may not always be completely divided. Through his extremely unjust and cruel actions in support of his murdering, lecherous brother, it turns out that a general amnesty is granted to prisoners, which must have freed many a poor soul from a grisly fate, for ancient punishments were harsh. Ts'ao himself has two sides, for while his conduct towards the wife of the dead scholar is wicked, he does it through his love for his brother rather than for personal gain. At a human level it illustrates the dilemmas of loyalty that may face us through being part of a family.

INNER ESSENCE

Li T'ieh-kuai also possesses life-giving qualities. His gourd that pours forth medicine to preserve life is a feminine symbol, suggesting the waters of the womb. Cycles of creation, womb to tomb and tomb to womb, are also evident for, like Chang-kuo, Li returns from the dead. The fact that he is left with the body of a beggar suggests that outward shape is of little significance when compared with the inner essence, so the spirit of an enlightened immortal could inhabit a twisted and filthy body.

SACRED FOOL

Lan Ts'ai-ho is the Sacred Fool of the pack. The Fool is often a symbol for spirituality, for he is divorced from the preoccupations of material life, and by his presence exerts a freeing influence on others. He inverts usual values. He represents the internal child within each of us. This part that plays freely with concepts that the conscious 'adult' mind may rigidly reject, may be a route to inspiration. The Fool also represents those parts of the personality that do not function efficiently or totally consciously, and with which we need to make friends. (This was why in medieval times the court jester was given pride of place beside the King.) In the myth there is no call upon Lan to behave sensibly or to take up a life of contemplation in order to obtain immortality: he simply finds it while drunk.

THE SINGLE FEMALE

Because Ho Hsien-ku is the sole female of the group, it is evident that within historical times Taoism was not a feminist religion, but was instead deeply patriarchal. Ho Hsien-ku gains her immortality in an 'Earth Mother' fashion, told in a dream and fashioned from the earth itself. The keys to spirit are found within matter. The six hairs on her head may have meaning arising within the ancient art of numerology, where numbers are assigned a quality. Six is a domestic, 'feminine' number connected with service, duty, devotion to ideals and family love. Her lotus flower reinforces this. The lotus represents the light of consciousness. A species of water lily, it resembles the moon reflected in the waters, in the same way that human nature, on earth, may be the reflection of the celestial. The water lily grows from mud and slimy substance into a thing of unparalleled beauty, in the same way that life and consciousness can transform the inert into something wonderful. The lotus is therefore another symbol of transformation.

Together, the Eight Immortals show how spiritual enlightenment is open to all people, from all walks of life, and can be approached in a variety of different ways.

The Feng Shui Master

In China the art of Feng Shui has long been respected, and Feng Shui masters are consulted regarding the sites of homes, temples and graveyards, because they understand all the subtle factors that affect a place, and are in tune with the earth energies. However, knowledge does not necessarily confer good temper, and such a master may, in some respects, be a very imperfect individual. One such was Wen Jeng.

Wen Jeng was well known throughout the countryside as being an expert authority on Feng Shui and he was much sought after for consultations. Sometimes these sent him far and wide, and as he was no longer a young man, he often found the journeys very tiresome. This in no way improved his temper, and he was often exhausted and resentful. One day he was asked to give his opinion on the site of a proposed grave, way up in the mountains.

It was a hot day and the way was long and arduous. Wen Jeng clambered over rocks in the blazing sun. At length he came to the spot and he took his readings and made notes. For a while he rested in the shade of an outcrop of rock, but the sun was high and powerful, and he had no water for his climb back down. The rest of the journey home would take several weeks and the village where he had spent the night lay in the wrong direction. Wen Jeng decided to set off home, but his legs felt weak, his head throbbed and his eyes were glazed from the brightness of the sun. Every time he swallowed, his throat rasped.

Slowly he made his way down the mountain, disturbing small boulders as he climbed, and coughing as the dust rose up around him. He became weaker and weaker and feared he would not make it home. He was no longer quite sure where he was. Indeed, he hardly cared what happened to him any more, for all he wanted was a drink of cool, clear water to soothe his parched throat, and a rest in the shade. But there seemed to be no shade anywhere, so Wen Jeng staggered on.

He was down the mountain now, and making his way across the plain, taking his direction from the sun, for his eyes were too caked with dust to look at his compass. Ahead of him he could see figures moving, and for a while he thought it must be a mirage, but as he approached, he began to hear the people talking. Then he knew they must be real. They took shape into a woman and her sons, winnowing grain. They stopped as he came close and he said to them, 'Please can you help me. Do you have water? I can't go for much longer without it.'

The woman came over to him and led him to the shade of a small tree, where Wen Jeng sprawled thankfully. Then she poured water from a pitcher she had kept in the shade into a bowl. Before she handed Wen Jeng the bowl she stooped and picked up a handful of chaff. This she sprinkled on top of the water, and offered it to the Feng Shui master.

He took it, desperate for the water, but without thanks. Even in his exhaustion he was furious that she had insulted him in this way. He blew through his teeth on the water, to disperse the chaff before each swallow. As he took down the cool draughts he planned to get his own back on the woman. His eyes began to clear and he looked about him. In the distance he could just see a shabby little shack.

'Is that your house?' he asked the woman.

'Yes,' she replied. 'It is falling down but I have no money to repair it. I and my three sons spend our days scratching for enough food. Three years ago my husband died and since then life has been nothing but struggle.'

'Ah,' said the Feng Shui master. 'Your troubles are now over. I am an expert in these matters and I can tell you that the positioning of your house has brought you bad luck. There is another site, across the mountains, an abandoned house that is yet in good repair. Move there with your sons – no one will stop you. Clear the creepers from the walls and the mountain rubble from the interior, and take up residence. Then the tide of fortune will turn in your favour.'

The woman and her sons knelt before him in gratitude. Now feeling much stronger and fortified by the cool water, Wen Jeng took up his bag and left. As he walked away he grunted to himself with satisfaction. For he had directed the woman to a dreadful place, where the Feng Shui was so bad that her children would probably die before reaching adulthood. It was a place the locals called 'Five Ghosts Dead Place'.

Several years later Wen Jeng again came to the mountains in order to pronounce on a site. He made a detour to visit the family, to see how the retribution he had planned was working out. He approached the house, which now looked neat and clean, with the fields around it tilled and fruitful. As he came close to the door, the woman rushed out and embraced him.

'Come in Great Master, come in,' she said. She ushered Wen Jeng to the honoured guest chair and went to get him some rice wine. As she did so, he looked about him. The house was homely and attractive. Hangings adorned the walls and a basket full of ripe fruit stood on the table. When the woman came back with the wine Wen Jeng asked her about her life.

'Everything is going so well, Master,' she said. 'The meeting with you changed our lives. Two of my sons are entering service with the government and the third is going for teaching with a Master. The fields are bountiful and we have excess produce to sell. I can even afford to have someone to help me in the fields when the boys leave. And this is all due to you, Master. If you had not come along that day, who can tell where we would all be now?' She kow-towed before him in gratitude.

Wen Jeng was amazed. He said little, but accepted the woman's invitation to partake of the evening meal with the family. The three sons came in from the fields, fine, well-grown and muscular young men, with perfect manners and intelligent speech. He was served well, with simple but nourishing fare, rice and fresh vegetables grown on the woman's land. At length, replete and relaxed, Wen Jeng sat back in his chair and said to the woman. 'Truly I cannot understand your good fortune. I sent you to the most inauspicious site I have ever encountered in all my career, and yet you have thrived and your family has prospered. What have you done, for Heaven to bless you so?'

The woman looked at him, surprised and dismayed. 'Master,' she said, 'Why would you do such a thing? How can this be?' She looked about her in confusion. 'All this, I thought it was your doing. And yet you tell me that you wished ill for me. What did I do to incur such displeasure?'

Wen Jeng lowered his head, slightly discomfited by her innocence. 'I came down from the mountains desperate for water. When I begged you for some you poured it for me, but then you threw chaff upon it, to insult me. Because of this I directed you to the worst place I knew.'

'How could you have been so mistaken?' asked the woman. 'When you came towards me you were spent and parched. I knew you were desperate for water, but the water I had brought from my well, in the pitcher, was very cold, and you were hot. You would have downed it all in an instant and it would have hit your stomach, giving you a great shock to your system. To protect you I sprinkled chaff upon the water, so that you would have to blow it aside each time you took a drink. In this way you drank the water slowly, and that was better for you.'

Wen Jeng could not help but smile. 'Despite the fact I sent you to this dire place,' he said, 'Heaven has blessed you and your sons. This is because you are so full of goodness that you have attracted good fortune. May you continue to be blessed, as you undoubtedly deserve.'

Commentary

This story has much of the gentle morality that we may think of as Chinese. It is a Taoist myth, but like several Taoist tales it mocks the precepts that are allied to Taoism.

FENG SHUI

Feng Shui (see also Appendix 1) is an Oriental system now fashionable in the West. It means 'Wind, Water' and is a way of arranging our surroundings in order to make our lives more harmonious and effectual. It is a complex and evolved system which is at least 5,000 years old. Many Chinese place great faith in Feng Shui, and it is partly because trading links are being developed with China that people in the West have developed an interest in it, because some Chinese regard it as essential for business. In Hong

Kong, Taiwan and Singapore it has always been employed. In China, Feng Shui was discouraged under the regime of Mao Tse Tung, but since the climate has become more relaxed it has returned rapidly to popularity.

Feng Shui is actually composed of several elements. Firstly it is based on something we may loosely call 'magical.' It resides on the borders between the seen and the unseen and works on the basis that these worlds interface. Thus circumstances can be brought about through symbols and associations, not through cause and effect. The subtle dynamics of a place can be altered, say, by the hanging of a wind-chime, thus the wind-chime could be seen as 'bringing good luck'. The unseen energy is called chi and this has similarities with other terms for life energy such as *prana* or *orgone*. While Feng Shui seeks to manipulate unseen forces, it is also passive because it uses surroundings and positioning as a form of divination, in order to ascertain the inner character of a place and what will happen there.

Feng Shui is also a philosophy, in that it teaches the interdependence of all things. A Feng Shui master will cast the horoscope of the people in a place in order to determine the sort of effect it will have upon them. Feng Shui rests within the concept of Taoism, the All, the Way, and the balance of Yin and Yang.

Lastly, Feng Shui rests upon the practical. It includes interior design, and places emphasis on the way that certain colours and shapes have an effect on the human being. One might argue that it is common sense, when buying a house, to enquire what happened to the former inhabitants. If all the couples that have lived previously in the house got divorced, or if several inhabitants have declined and died in quick succession, one might justifiably wonder whether there was some negative energy attached to it.

Feng Shui is fundamental to Taoist belief and Chinese culture. It is deeply rooted in their belief system but also important on a practical level. There is no real parallel with it in the West. Only by understanding a little about Feng Shui can we appreciate the power of the Feng Shui master and the respect he commanded.

MENTAL SYSTEMS

Feng Shui, however esoteric its origins, is a system developed by the conscious mind. It is complex, being full of rules and regulations.

However questionable we may consider its scientific basis, there is no mistaking the rational nature of the construct. The myth clearly tells us that all of this only goes so far. In the end it is what you are, not what you do, that determines your destiny. Fate cannot be cheated, and character is Fate, something with which many psychologists of the twentieth century would agree. Our character unconsciously moulds our destiny. In the case of the woman in the myth, her compassionate and considerate nature and her innocence attracted the good fortune that Feng Shui proscribed.

THE MASTER WAS WRONG

The Feng Shui master got it wrong when it came to determining this woman's future. One tends to feel that he deserved some retribution himself for his bitter vengefulness – for he would have jeopardized the lives of the children because of a 'discourtesy'. But, in a way, he gets his deserts because all his fine systems and his wisdom are set at naught by the woman's goodness, which conquered everything.

APPLYING THE MYTH

For us the myth has a simple but profound application. It teaches us to have faith in our inner nature, rather than attempt to control everything. Even the 'alternative' scene with its esoteric systems could be seen as another, subtler, form of control in a culture that seeks to overcome not only the material world, but also the spiritual one. The fact that the Feng Shui master comes to no harm indicates that such attempts are not wrong in themselves. What the story tells us is that no single system of science or philosophy holds the final answer.

9

Wen Chang, God of Literature

The official history of Wen Chang starts with an individual called Chang Ya, who lived in Szechuan 618–906 CE. He was employed on the Board of Rites where he held a post of great responsibility and authority, but one day he simply disappeared. After this he became something of a saint and was posthumously awarded many accolades. He became identified with Chang Ya-tzu, killed in a fight in the third or fourth century. As time went by he was credited with increasingly legendary gifts, his exploits extending further back into the mists of antiquity. But who can explain the ways of the gods? Wen Chang comes to earth at intervals when he is needed by the people. His gift is wisdom, and he is sometimes a teacher.

The first time Wen Chang appeared was about 3000 years ago, in ancient Shu, which is now Sichuan. This was fertile ground, and roused much envy in neighbouring rulers, the most sinister of which was the Lord of Chin. But the people of Shu had many spies and fierce armies, and he could find no way to impose his rule or infiltrate their domains, so he summoned his counsel, and a wise man advised him.

'Great Lord, the king of Shu has a son of marriageable age. Offer to him the hand of your daughter, and those in Shu will regard you as a friend, and their watchfulness will cease.'

The king feared to send his daughter into danger, but the wise man went on, 'Send with her a retinue of your finest fighting men as her attendants. When the people of Shu are at their most welcoming, then they will be most vulnerable. And you, my Lord, will have a contingent of your finest warriors already in their midst.'

Convinced by the cleverness of the plan, the king sent emissaries to Shu, offering friendship, and his daughter as the wife of the prince. All in Shu were delighted at the prospect of peace, and matters were set in hand for a magnificent state wedding. The young woman was in her chamber preparing for the wedding when Wen Chang came to her. He did not come in human form, but as a mighty snake. The girl screamed and ran from the palace in a panic, and all her attendants and retinue ran with her. When they were all well clear of the palace, the god Wen Chang took hold of a great mountain and brought it down on top of them all, killing them. This mountain is called Tzu Ku, and on its crest is the temple of Wen Chang, worshipped in his manifestation as Thunder God.

Wen Chang then disappeared from human view, but he reappeared many more times when needed, and one of his most notable visits was again to the province of Sichuan in 1000 CE. A rebel lord, one Wang Chun, had occupied the capital of Sichuan, Chengdu, and had based his troops there to revolt against the rightful Sung dynasty. The Emperor sent armies to retake the capital, but all to no avail, as the rebels derided them from the city walls. The general tried to persuade the city to surrender by promising the rebels a general amnesty, and this he communicated by sending messages attached to arrows, which were shot over the city walls and among the rebels in the streets. But nothing would shift the rebels and the city remained impregnable.

Then, from among the crowd, a man emerged and climbed a ladder. Standing above the throng, he proclaimed that he bore a message from Wen Chang himself, and that the city was destined to fall to the besiegers on the twentieth day of the ninth month, and that none should escape alive. Many who heard tried to shout him down and shake him from his post, but he stood firm. Then the soldiers shot arrows at him, but despite the fact that their aim was good, it seemed that nothing could touch him. He continued to prophesy until his words were finished, and then he simply disappeared. Just as foretold, the city did indeed fall to the general, and not one rebel escaped alive. In honour of his intervention, the victorious general ordered that his temple be repaired and due obeisance and sacrifice made to the god.

In common with all officials, Wen Chang had a colleague, and they are both marked in the sky, in the Great Bear. Like Wen Chang, he is reputed to have actually lived upon earth. He was born in ancient China, into a peasant family who scraped a living from the earth. Truth to tell, he was hideously ugly, so ugly that many of the villagers averted their faces when he drew near, but his parents loved him, and under their guidance he grew up intelligent and wise. Indeed, it was soon obvious that his mental powers were exceptional, and that despite his personal appearance he had a bright and kindly soul. His name was Chung Kuei, and as he grew he studied, working night and day until he worked his way through all the local examinations. Eventually he was in a position to travel to the Imperial City and sat the examinations there, in which he came first.

Each year the student who came first in these prestigious examinations was personally awarded a golden rose by the Emperor himself, and, in pride and excitement, Chung Kuei prepared himself for the audience. However, as he went into the presence chamber, the Emperor caught sight of his dreadful countenance and immediately ordered that he be taken out of his sight, so frightful did he look. Chung Kuei, dashed from the heights to the depths, saw his life before him as one of disgrace and humiliation. Despite all his efforts he was banished.

How could he now return home to his hard-working parents and tell them of his rejection? Despairing, he rushed for the seashore and cast himself into the waves, wishing to be drowned as quickly as possible. But the gods on high who had been watching his progress, and who were well pleased with him, decreed that this fate was unfair, and sent a sea monster to his rescue. As he was about to succumb to the enveloping waters, this creature issued from the depths and supported him on its nose. It continued to rise, lifting him up, up, out of the sea, over the waves and the clouds, and into the stars beyond. Chung Kuei was given the stewardship of all those who study, and along with Wen Chang he looks after officials and scholars.

A third individual also enters the picture, and he, too, through his virtues, is part of the heavenly Ministry of Education. His name is Lu Chi, and he lived in the time of the Tang dynasty, 618–907 CE, and from an early age he seemed to have exceptional qualities. The divine princess Tai Yin spotted him, and, taken by his beauty, his intelligence and his industry, she desired to marry him.

Accordingly the High Gods arranged to transport Lu Chi into Heaven for a meeting. He was offered three possible futures: he could marry the princess, who stood before him in all her heavenly beauty, and become an immortal, staying in her palace among the gods; he could go back to earth and live there as an immortal; or he could simply return to earth as a human, and work his way upwards, so having a chance to help others.

What could Lu Chi say? Seduced by the dazzling goddess he chose to stay and be with her. The princess was delighted and the Jade Emperor was duly informed. The Emperor decided to allow some time to elapse before ratifying the matter, and made arrangements to send a messenger at a later date to see how Lu Chi felt. When the messenger arrived Lu Chi did not answer, for now his mind was full of doubts. Still, the lovely princess held on his arm and begged him to stay. Again the messenger asked, and Lu Chi at length told him that he wished to become a minister in the Imperial Court, in order to serve the people.

He was then taken back to earth, where he studied even harder than before. On taking the Imperial exam, he achieved the highest mark, and after some years of service he became a minister. After a long life of diligent service, his time came to die whereupon his head turned into that of a panther, his lips became dragon-lips and he turned blue, which is the colour of the Immortals. Many watched as he rose bodily into Heaven.

Commentary

This myth is included partly because it illustrates some of the complexities inherent in Chinese myth-making.

THE HEAVENLY HIERARCHY

Wen Chang is a good example of a ubiquitous god, respected by Confucians and others. The Chinese heavenly system mirrors that of earth, and Wen Chang is one of many ministers, who, under the Jade Emperor and the Queen Mother of the West, administer existence. There are hundreds of similar deities, ranging from gods of thunder, through smallpox, war, hell and more positive subjects such as medicine. Regional gods are ranged beneath them, and every city, town and region has its personal deity; even private houses each have several gods in residence, for the kitchen, hearth etc. Thus China is a polytheistic culture.

Although K'ung Fu-tzu, or Confucius, receives most veneration, Wen Chang seems to be an earlier figure, dating from before 500 BCE. He usually comes to earth when called, and 17 such visits are recorded in legend. He is represented in a constellation of six stars, near the Great Bear.

SACRED LANDSCAPE

The story gives a legendary reason for a part of the landscape. This is also the case in 'The Dragon's Pearl' (Tales of Dragons, Chapter 12). It is a common theme in many cultures and is most notable in the Songlines of the Aborigines, where the landscape has a kind of simultaneous existence in fact and legend and is brought to life by recounting the legends. By this process human beings maintain a living connection with the environment which, according to some theories, is affected by thought. This approach is now being endorsed by quantum physics, where the presence or otherwise of the viewer affects the outcome of the experiment.

SHAMANIC ASSOCIATIONS

Lu Chi at his death shows animal characteristics, indicating as in so many of the stories shamanistic ideas of power animals. The animals incorporated into his appearance say much about his eloquence and wisdom (the dragon's lips) and his strength and courage (the panther's head). The colour blue, which is that of the sky, refers to the inner essence of the spirit.

WEN CHANG AS A SNAKE

The snake has many associations, from ineffable wisdom to treachery. Specifically, its spiralling coils represent the transformation process into and out of the spirit world. Thus it is linked with the process of initiation and inner awakening. It is also associated with sexuality. Being close to the source of life, it symbolizes something deep within the unconscious. It is at once inhuman and sublime, representing the cold-blooded essence of the reptile, the worm of decay and also the transcendence available through the instincts. It also has links with the Ancestors.

In the story the snake pinpoints the wrongful use of sexuality, in that the princess is used to increase her father's power. The snake embodies the power of the land that rises up to reject a ruler that is not rightful. (This is similar to the Celtic belief that the king ruled the land by mandate of the goddess, who represented it.) As the traitors flee, they are engulfed by the land itself in the shape of a mountain. The theme of 'rightful ruler' is echoed in the second tale, although we may be sure that this was used to press the political claims of individuals as being 'chosen'.

The sea monster that appears to rescue Chung Kuei is also reminiscent of the reptilian snake. In reality this is a 'winged snake' that represents the higher and lower aspects of human nature and how one can rise through the other. The final story contains no such symbolism, but some of the themes can be discerned in the behaviour of Lu Chi. He is selected for immortality essentially because of his sexual attractiveness to the goddess, and although he elects to return to earth, eventually he does become immortal (and one wonders if the goddess is waiting!). He brings his gift of wisdom back down to earth in order to help others rise. Here is a theme of the triumphant union of mind with matter. The continued power and presence of the instinctual elements are indicated by the dragon-lips and panther head of Lu Chi.

HEAVENLY REWARDS

Many myths promise heavenly rewards for virtue, and the story of Chung Kuei is an example of this. Such stories serve to console those who experience misfortune in life. They are a promise of better things to come and indicate that the universe is fundamentally just. This view has similarities to the belief in karma, which concerns the law of cause and effect, although it is often misunderstood as a system of justice and retribution.

10

The Silkworm Goddess

In ancient China there once lived a girl who was often lonely.
Her father was away continually on business, and she missed him
dreadfully. One day, while grooming her horse, she whispered to him
how much she missed her father.

'How I wish he was here, to talk to me, comfort me and keep me
company,' she sighed. 'The truth is I would marry anyone who
brought my father back to me.'

To her surprise the horse reared and shook off her hand. As she
stepped back, he wheeled away and bolted out of the yard. She
sadly assumed that he, too, had left her, and went back to her
household duties.

Meanwhile, in a far-off part of the country, the father was disturbed
at his work by a loud neighing and stamping of hooves. He put
down his quill and went to investigate. There was his horse, making
as much clamour as it could. Immediately he became very anxious.
Hardly giving himself time to say goodbye to his colleagues, he leapt
astride the horse and galloped off in the direction of his home. He
assumed something serious must be amiss with his daughter, and was
filled with apprehension until he saw her at the door, her face full of
surprise and delight.

'Why did the horse come to find me?' asked the father.

'I do not know, except that I told him I missed you, and he must
have understood.'

For the next few days the horse was treated with special care, and
given the best fodder and stabling, but he appeared unsettled and
didn't touch his food. The only time he seemed to have any life in him

was when the young woman came near to him, when he would rear up, whinny and nuzzle her. No one could understand why the horse was behaving so strangely, until the young woman remembered her remark, while grooming him.

'It may be, Father,' she said, 'that the horse remembers that I said I would marry the person who brought you home to me.'

'But he is a beast!' cried the father. 'How can that be?' In outrage and fury, he went to the stables, took out his sword and killed the horse. Then he skinned it and hung the hide out in the sun, to dry.

The next day the young woman was outside her home, in the sunshine, talking with her friends. She pointed out the skin and laughed at it, whereupon it flew into the air, swooped at her and wound itself around her. Then it carried her off, out of the sight of her amazed friends. They called her father, and he and the neighbours searched long and desperately for the girl, until they almost gave up all hope of finding her alive. Tired and despairing, they were about to set off for home when they spotted her in the branches of a mulberry tree, still wrapped in the skin of the horse. But she was no longer the same. Her body had altered to that of a strange worm-like being, and her head was the shape of a horse's head. From this was emerging an endless thread of white silk, with which she was cocooning herself. The girl had turned into the silkworm goddess.

The August Personage of Jade looked down from Heaven, and seeing the poor girl within the tree he took pity on her. He lifted her up into Heaven, where she became one of his concubines, known as Lady Horse-Head. And so the silkworm goddess came into being. Later in time she came down from heaven and gave the Yellow Emperor a gift of silk. With this he was so pleased that he and his wife decided to cultivate it. And so the silk industry was given to China.

Commentary

This is a traditional Chinese folk tale, dating back to the era of King Kao H'sin-shih, 2436–2366 BCE. The silkworm lady is known as Ts'an Nu, but three other deities are also known by the same name. She is also known as Ma-t'ou Niang, or Horse-Head Lady, and images of her are worshipped on the third day of the third month.

Prayers are made for the cultivation of mulberry trees and the successful rearing of silkworms.

SILK

At a cultural and practical level, this myth is about the early beginnings of the silk industry, which was, and still is, so important to China. For many centuries spices and silk were the most valuable trading assets the Chinese possessed, and they were taken to the West along the Silk Road. China is still one of the largest silk-producing nations in the world. Silk-spinning began there as long ago as 1200 BCE, at a time when such gifts would have been prized as gifts of the gods and a prime subject for the weaving of tales. However, the myth has several meanings in addition to this.

The silkworm goddess is part of a very ancient tradition of spinning and weaving goddesses, who were often major creatrix figures. The web of life is an image of the cosmos with its multiplicity of interdependent factors, and each thread is a metaphor for individual life. China has always been a very patriarchal country, and we can only speculate about earlier, matriarchal traditions. There seems, however, to be a connection with the ancient goddess in the symbolism of the mulberry tree. The three phases of the ripening of the mulberry berries are white, red and black, and these have associations with the Triple Goddess – maiden, mother and crone – and with the three stages of life – childhood, adulthood and old age. It is also linked with industry and filial piety, beloved of the Chinese.

THE HORSE

Perhaps the most important symbolic figure in the tale is that of the horse. Horses were prized animals in earlier times. In medieval Europe, for instance, a nobleman would value his horse above a whole village of peasants, because the horse gave him the means to get about, rather like our motor cars today. The horse is an animal of great power, signifying energy on many levels. This can be the energy of true instinct, which carries people along more quickly than the conscious mind, or it may be the energy of the passions, the animal urges, which are at odds with the ego, or conscious, rational aspect. The horse is also an Underworld figure, in that it represents the darker aspects of the psyche, and in many mythologies is the mount for Death. In this myth it is the animal lusts which are the interesting component.

FATHER FIXATION

We meet the young woman at the start of the story quite obsessed with her father. Incest is not implied, but her immature fixation on her father means that the normal development of her womanly passions is arrested. The erotic component of her love for her father, which cannot be expressed because of the incest-fear, is symbolized by the horse, to which she confides her longing. At the same time she is unconsciously seeking to leave that fear behind and experience desire for a man of her own age.

It is tempting to imagine another end to the story. If the girl had gone out to the stable, put her arms around the horse and promised to marry it, would it then have transformed into a handsome young man? Instead, the father goes out and kills the horse. The possessive aspect of the father kills off the development of his daughter's adult passions. He then hangs the horsehide out to dry in the sun. In Chinese symbolism, the Yang of the sunlight drives out the Yin of the moisture. This is victory for the rational mind over the instincts, masculine over feminine, but it is also a recipe for disaster. The passions cannot so easily be vanquished and 'dried out', and as the girl mocks the hide, it leaps from the posts on which it is strung out and carries her away. She loses her humanity and all possibility of becoming an adult woman – instead she turns into a creature of the most basic kind, a silkworm. This primitive creature is actually extremely productive and creative, and this fact is marked by the way in which the Jade Emperor intervenes. The seed of creativity is still present and with it the possibility of redemption.

11

Monkey King

Once there was a rock that had lain between Earth and Heaven, since the creation of the world. Sunlight and moonlight fell upon it, until it became magically pregnant and, at length, split open to reveal a stone egg. The winds fed this egg until it grew legs and arms and eventually took shape as a stone monkey. The first thing this monkey did was to bow in the direction of each of the four points directions of the compass. So doing, a steely light flashed from its eyes as far as the Cloud Palace of the August Personage of Jade. The Jade Emperor sent his captains to investigate, and they reported the birth of the stone monkey. However, the Emperor was not surprised, for the creatures on Earth were made of the essences both of Heaven and Earth, and their doings could not be foretold, even by the gods.

The stone monkey leapt and played with the other monkeys. One day they all followed a stream to where it surged down from the rocks in a great waterfall. The monkeys all cried out that if anyone were brave enough to go behind the curtain of water, he should be king. The stone monkey volunteered, and leapt through the rushing water. Inside he found another world, where flowers and trees grew and where there were dwellings furnished with stone cups and plates and with everything they could desire. The monkeys were overjoyed and excited. One by one, with their old ones and their children, they went through the water-curtain into the new country. The stone monkey reminded them of their promise, and they acclaimed him Monkey King. They lived long and happily, but at length Monkey King became sad, and when his ministers asked him why, he said that it was because one day he would die.

His ministers gathered about him and gave him advice. They said that certain people were exempt from the Wheel of Rebirth, and

Figure 11.1 Monkey King

that instruction could be found for Monkey King so that he could join them. Excited, he made plans to leave. He journeyed for many a long year, leaving behind his monkey companions, but he found no Immortals. One day, as he ventured through a wood, he heard a woodcutter singing about the immortals that he had encountered. Monkey King begged him to explain, and the woodcutter said that indeed a sage lived close by, but he himself was not able to study with him because he had to look after his aged mother. So Monkey King journeyed on, alone, until he found the cave of the sage, as explained by the woodcutter. There he was laughed at, but stood his ground nonchalantly. The patriarch bestowed upon him the name 'Aware-of-Vacuity' and agreed that he could study with him.

After much instruction and many mistakes, strange to tell, the Monkey King gained enlightenment and indeed became immortal.

* * *

Monkey King returned to his monkey subjects, who were all overjoyed to see him. They skipped and danced about him.

However, Monkey was no longer content merely to be king of the monkeys, and he embarked on many exploits, challenging even the Jade Emperor himself. No one could stop him, and even the mightiest of the heavenly captains fell before him.

At length he was given the title 'Great Sage, Equal of Heaven' but still he misbehaved. He stole the Elixir of Life, ate the Peaches of Immortality and drank the Wine of Heaven. He was captured and brought to the place of execution, where heavenly soldiers began to hew at him with axes, but all to no avail. Fire and thunderbolts were equally ineffectual. So Lao Tzu came forward and offered to place him in the Crucible of the Eight Trigrams and reduce him to ashes with alchemical fire. However, this was not successful, for Monkey emerged from the crucible unharmed, except for his eyes which had turned fiery red.

After that a terrific battle ensued which was so bad that even the Jade Emperor was alarmed. As there seemed to be nothing within the Taoist heavenly court that could defeat Monkey King, the Emperor sent for the Buddha.

The Buddha came to Monkey and spoke to him, asking what he wanted. He learned from Monkey that he had been sent to challenge the August Personage of Jade himself. The Buddha laughed out loud at this seeming impudence and asked him what magic he had, that enabled him to issue so enormous a challenge.

'I can transform into 72 different shapes and can somersault through the clouds 180,000 leagues in one leap,' he replied. The Buddha laughed again.

'I will make a bargain with you,' he said. 'Show me that you can leap off my right palm. Do this and I will take the Jade Emperor to live with me in the Western Paradise, and leave you to reign in his stead. But if you do not succeed you must return to Earth and do penance.'

'Fine – I accept,' said Monkey, thinking the Buddha a fool, for his palm was the size of a lotus leaf. He stood on it and jumped, flying through the air for an immense distance. At last he came to a place where there were five pink pillars stretching up into the sky. 'This is obviously the end of the world,' said Monkey King to himself. 'But I had better leave proof of my being here in case the Buddha proves troublesome. He plucked a hair from his head, breathed on it so that it changed to a pen and wrote on the base of one of the pillars, 'Here passed the Great Sage, Equal of Heaven'. Then he relieved himself at the base of one of the other pillars and went winging back, to claim his reward. He stood on the palm of the Buddha and proclaimed his victory.

'Smelly ape,' said the Buddha. 'All this time you have been on the palm of my hand.'

'No, no,' replied Monkey. 'I went to the end of the world and wrote something on one of the great pillars that rises there. Come with me and I'll show you.'

'No need,' laughed the Buddha, 'Just look.'

Monkey did as he was told, and there, on one of the fingers of the Buddha were written the words 'Here passed the Great Sage Equal of Heaven'. He looked further, and there at the base of another finger was a puddle smelling of Monkey's urine.

Monkey could not believe what he saw and was getting ready to spring again when the Buddha pushed him out of Heaven. As he did this he changed his five fingers into the five elements, Metal, Wood, Water, Fire and Earth. These became a five-peaked mountain that pressed down over Monkey and captured him. The Jade Emperor returned and showered the Buddha with thanks and there was rejoicing in Heaven. Monkey King was spotted raising his head through the mountains, whereupon the Buddha drew from his sleeve a seal on which were inscribed the words 'Om Mani Padme Hum'. This was stamped hard upon the top of the five peaks. They sealed together, allowing enough air to breathe, but nothing more, and so the Stone Monkey was thoroughly imprisoned.

And so began his long penance until he was at length rescued.

* * *

Five hundred years later it happened that the great Emperor of T'ang was visited by the Boddhisattva, Kuan Yin. Following this he was inspired to send to India for the holy Buddhist scriptures. The man chosen for the mission was a priest called Hsuan Tsang, but he was renamed Tripitaka, after the scriptures themselves contained in three baskets. Tripitaka, however, soon encountered dangers and obstacles in his path, and because of this Monkey was released to help him with his mission. Other helpers also came on the journey. A minister from the court of the Jade Emperor had been banished for misconduct and was reborn from the womb of a pig. Because of this he was very ugly, and stupid and lazy into the bargain. He was induced to come along and help the party, and called Pigsy. Sandy, another pilgrim, was also once a heavenly minister, but he was reborn into the body of a shark. Tripitaka had a white horse, who had once been a dragon, and who had eaten Tripitaka's original mount. It was given the job of carrying Tripitaka as a penance. This motley crew took off to brave the dangers of the wilderness and to bring the holy scriptures to the Emperor's court, and on the way they had many strange adventures.

* * *

Having encountered many perils, the party were enjoying a peaceful interlude when they began to hear an awful noise, like stones scraping down a hillside. As they came over the brow of a hill a sight met their eyes that was most unwelcome. It was a crowd of Buddhist monks dragging a cart up a narrow pass, and calling on divine names to help their miserable task. Nearby, there stood a city, and as two Taoist monks came out of the city gates, the monks redoubled their efforts, as if terrified. Monkey decided to investigate further, and, being master of disguise, this was no problem for him. He changed himself into a Taoist monk and came towards the two Taoists, chanting songs and shaking his tambourine.

'Pray, brothers, tell me where I may beg for bread for my supper.'

'Beg?' asked the Taoists, in surprise. 'We can see that you are new to these lands. This country is called Cart Slow and we Taoists are supreme here. Twenty years ago there was a terrible famine here, and although the people prayed for rain none fell until three mighty Immortals came to us, and saved us. Their names are Tiger Strength, Deer Strength and Ram Strength.'

'Please do me the honour of taking me to meet these august individuals,' supplicated Monkey, laughing up his sleeve.

'Soon, brother, but first we must check what those Buddhists are doing. They proved themselves imposters when they could not help the drought that caused the famine. Their passports were taken from them so they might not flee, and they do penance by acting as our servants.'

'Alas,' cried Monkey, laughing up his sleeve again. 'I have come to seek my uncle, who was a Buddhist. Can it be that he is among the bondsmen?'

'Friend,' replied the Taoists, 'as you are a Taoist yourself, you are welcome to go up to the Buddhists and check for the presence of your uncle.'

So Monkey made his way to the Buddhists, who cringed at first, as if they expected to be beaten. Seeing Monkey wished them only well, they began to answer his questions and to tell him about the three Immortals.

'They can make the philosopher's stone, turn stones into gold and water into oil. They are magicians indeed.'

'Ah, but I know one who is better,' smiled Monkey. He set off back towards the Taoists and told them that all the monks were his kinsmen. When they refused to release them at once he did what he, Monkey, did best. He brought out his cudgel and slew them on the spot.

The Buddhists wailed with fright, and when Monkey explained that he had come to save them, they told him that they had dreamed of their saviour, and that he had steely eyes a flat forehead and hairy cheeks. Monkey laughed again and resumed his true form, whereupon the Buddhists recognized him, and rejoiced. He now released all of them.

Meanwhile the rest of the party were waiting for him. With a handful of monks who had decided to stay, Monkey ushered the group into the temple. Outside there was an uproar and Monkey and Pigsy went to investigate. A Taoist ritual was in progress and at the centre of it were the three Immortals they had all heard about. Pigsy wanted to rush at the bowls of fruits and viands, but Monkey restrained him.

'Leave this to me,' he said, and filling his cheeks with air he blew so hard upon the Taoists that they thought a great wind had come upon them, and Tiger Strength told them all to go. The place was soon deserted and the three adventurers were about to settle down to enjoy the banquet when Monkey had an idea. He spotted statues of the Taoist Trinity, the Great Primordial, the Lord of the Sacred Treasures and Lao Tzu. Monkey told Pigsy to take the three images into a side room used for 'metabolic transmigration', which Pigsy discovered to be a toilet. He deposited the images there, laughing at the cleverness of Monkey, and came back all splashed with filth. He took the place of Lao Tzu while Monkey took that of the Great Primordial, and Sandy the place of the Lord of the Sacred Treasures.

Sandy and Pigsy were starving and proceeded to devour the banquet, dumplings, rice-balls, cakes and fruits of all descriptions, while Monkey ate a few nuts and some of the fruits. Soon all the food was gone, as if a cloud of locusts had passed. Replete and relaxed, the three fell to joking and laughing. As luck would have it, a little Taoist awoke from his sleep and recalled that he had left his small hand-bell in the temple. Afraid of getting into trouble with his elders, he decided to creep back to look for it. He found it, and was about to slink back to his bed when he heard the sound of breathing. Terrified, he dropped his bell, whereupon Pigsy couldn't help bursting into loud laughter. The little Taoist ran from the temple as fast as his heels could carry him, straight back to his master. The three Immortals were there, too, and he told them breathlessly how the temple had been possessed by some evil spirit. They all found torches, and approached the temple to investigate.

Monkey, Pigsy and Sandy sat still as stone while the Taoists looked about them.

'Surely', cried Ram Strength, 'the Great Ones have themselves come to eat our offerings. Let us pray for the Heavenly Elixir,' and the Taoists fell to reciting scriptures, and dancing a ritual dance. Monkey spoke in a grave voice, telling them to procure receptacles and they bustled off to find three pots.

'Now go,' commanded Monkey, 'for no one shall witness our Mysteries.' So the Taoists went out of the temple, and Monkey, Sandy and Pigsy passed water into each of the pots. When the Taoists returned they could not wait to drink of the Water of Immortality, but Ram Strength remarked that it tasted like pig's urine. Seeing that the game was up, Monkey let out a great laugh, and taking hold of his two companions, one in each hand, he leapt upon his cloud and all three returned to where Tripitaka waited.

The four travellers presented themselves at court the following day, where the King, hearing of their mission and not wanting to be on bad terms with China, would have given them safe passage. But the three Immortals spoke out against this, telling of their misdeeds. The King flew into a rage and would have executed them on the spot, but Monkey intervened with clever words. 'How could we have known our way to the temple, in the dark?' he enquired. 'Your Majesty, we are strangers here. Clearly, for some reason, these Taoists are framing us.' Now the King was no statesman, and he was confused. As he stroked his beard and reflected, a group of village elders were admitted, asking that something be done about the drought, for no rain had fallen in many months.

'Ah,' said the King. 'It was because you Buddhists could not make rain that you were suppressed. Now you shall have a competition. Let us see who can make the best rain, your four priests or my three Immortals.'

A great altar was erected, around which the banners of the 28 lunar mansions were unfurled. Torches blazed and incense burned. Deer Strength Immortal advanced to the altar, with his sword outstretched and uttering incantations. As he spoke the wind began to blow and the clouds gathered. Seeing this, Monkey leapt into the air and sped to the home of the Weather Gods. The Old Woman of the Wind, the Thunder God and the Mother of Lightning saw him approach, and held back to hear his bidding.

'This magic is valid,' they said. 'The Jade Emperor has sent us to make a storm. What say you, Father?'

'Make the storm, my friends,' said Monkey, 'but wait until I give the signal.'

They kow-towed to Monkey and agreed to watch for the signal that he would give with his cudgel. Having obtained their agreement, Monkey returned to Earth, where Deer Strength had unbound his hair, and was reciting scriptures in a loud voice and waving his sword like a maniac. But the sky remained clear, the air still, and no rain fell.

'Now, your Majesty, it is my turn,' cried Monkey. As Tripitaka prayed, Monkey pointed his cudgel towards the sky and immediately the wind whipped the 28 banners, the sky grew dark and the sound of a mighty rushing was heard, as the rain deluged from the heavens. But the Taoists were not discomfited, and they claimed credit, saying that the four dragons stood by in the Heavens and there had merely been a delay in their request getting through. Now the poor King was utterly confused, but Monkey stepped up and offered to summon the dragons into his presence. Not to be outdone, the Taoists also claimed they could summon the dragons, but all their spells were to no avail. They could only leave Monkey to take his turn, and he summoned the great ones with a loud voice. In the four corners of Heaven the dragons now appeared, and all the assembled company fell to their knees, as the King burned incense and prayed. And so the great ones of the Heavens remained until Monkey dismissed them, and the victory of the four pilgrims over the Taoists was complete.

* * *

Now the King would have stamped their passports and let them leave, but the Immortals came before him and reminded him of their long service, requesting that another competition be arranged, and this time it would be a contest of meditation. On hearing this Monkey was cast down, for although he could fly across the skies, move the stars and control the weather, sitting still was something he could not do.

'Friend,' said Tripitaka, 'be of good cheer. I am a Master of meditation and can remain suspended between life and death for three years.' And so the contest was begun, with Tiger Strength Immortal levitating to the top of his meditation tower, and Monkey carrying Tripitaka to his, on his magic cloud. There they remained, motionless, and it seemed neither would win, but one of the other Immortals grew impatient and fashioned a louse from the hairs on his neck, sending this to bite Tripitaka. The sting of this was unbearable, and Tripitaka began to twitch. Monkey, seeing this, took on the form of a gnat and brushed off the louse. He flew over to the Immortal and turned into a centipede, which burrowed into his ear, causing the Immortal to cry out and fall. Tripitaka was the undisputed winner of this contest, and it seemed the four would be released, but Deer Strength approached, claiming that his brother had been afflicted by a chill. He challenged the pilgrims to another contest, of 'guessing what's within', and Monkey agreed, without hesitation. Preparation was made for the third challenge.

A coffer was brought from the Queen's apartments, in which she had secreted a fine robe. Monkey turned into a gnat and went inside the casket, turning the robe into a cracked dish. Deer Strength came forward and pronounced that a royal robe was within, but, prompted by Monkey, Tripitaka said that it was a cracked dish. The King would have executed him on the spot but Monkey insisted that the box be opened, whereupon the old dish was brought forward, and the poor Queen discredited. Enraged, the King decided that he would place the next object within the coffer himself, and he plucked a ripe peach, which he put upon the red satin of the interior. Monkey went within and ate the peach, with great enjoyment. Ram Strength guessed there was a peach inside, and Tripitaka was afraid to argue, lest he be put to death.

'Trust me,' urged Monkey. 'Within there is only a peach stone.' And so it was, and Ram Strength retired, bewildered.

Tiger Strength now reappeared and asked for his turn. So within the coffer was placed a small boy who was a Taoist acolyte. Monkey again used his magic, and the boy emerged with his head shaven, reciting Buddhist scriptures, and it was as Tripitaka had said, not as Tiger Strength had guessed. The four pilgrims were victorious for the third time, and the assembled crowd burst into applause. The three Immortals stood, heads bowed, but they were still not prepared to admit defeat. They consulted together and came forward to the King with a terrifying request.

* * *

'Your Majesty,' began Tiger Strength, 'this competition has been beneath us. When we were young we learned arts that these fools cannot match. My head can be cut off and I can replace it, Deer Strength's heart can be torn out and he can be healed, and Ram Strength can bathe unscathed in boiling oil. We challenge the newcomers to submit to the same tests.'

The King shook his head, for truth to tell he was a little afraid of the outcome. Pigsy, hearing what was going on, came to Monkey in terror, but Monkey laughed out loud. He strode up to the King and said, 'I will take up the challenge of the three Immortals. You may cut off my head, rip out my heart and throw me into a cauldron of boiling oil, and I shall be fit and well.'

'Fellow,' said the King, 'you know not to what you submit yourself.'
But Tiger Strength stepped forward, saying, 'The challenge has been issued and taken up. Your Majesty, do not dissuade him.'

So Monkey was bound hand and foot and led to the place of execution, where 3,000 soldiers of the royal guard stood to attention. The executioner lifted his great sword and at the word 'Strike' it scythed through the air and Monkey's head sprang from his neck and rolled down the slope for 30 paces. Then a voice issued from Monkey's trunk calling 'Head, come back to me.' But this was heard by Deer Strength, who called on the gods of hill and dale to prevent the return of the head, and Monkey stood, headless. But then, from out of his neck, a new head was seen to sprout and he burst his bonds. The King pronounced that he should go free.

'Indeed,' cried Monkey, 'but the trial is not complete. Let the Immortal now take his turn.'

So Tiger Strength mounted the scaffold and his head in turn was sliced from his shoulders. And he now called to the head to come back, but Monkey took a hair from his head, blew upon it and it became a brown dog, who took the head away in its jaws and dropped it into the moat. Although Tiger Strength called and called, the head did not come back. Blood spurted from his neck in a great fount and he fell to the earth, dead. All that those watching could now see was the headless corpse of an enormous tiger.

The King turned pale as death but the remaining Immortals were unperturbed. 'My brother may be dead,' conceded Deer Strength, 'but the tiger lying there is merely some trick of this ruffian. I now challenge him to belly-ripping.'

Accordingly Monkey was led back to the scaffold and his belly cut open, whereupon he calmly examined his guts, placed them back inside and blew upon the wound, so that it closed. The King trembled to ask Deer Strength to submit, but the Immortal went confidently to the place of execution. His belly, in turn, was ripped open, but as he made to push his guts back inside, Monkey plucked a hair and blew upon it, changing it into a hawk, which swooped upon the exposed intestines and flew off with them to make a meal of them. Deer Strength collapsed and, tied to the stake, all that those who watched could now see was the corpse of a white deer.

The King looked in fear at Ram Strength, who denied that the corpse of the deer had anything to do with his brother. 'Light the fires,' he commanded, 'for the contest is not yet over.' The fires were lit beneath a huge cauldron of oil, which slowly began to boil and bubble. 'Ah,' said Monkey, scratching his back, 'I do so need a bath. May I take my turn first?' So saying he pulled off his attire and leapt into the boiling oil where he splashed and played like a fish in water. Pigsy and Sandy whispered together that they had never taken him seriously enough and that his powers were very great, but Monkey thought they were making fun of him. So, determined to get his own back, he changed into a tin tack, sank to the bottom of the cauldron and disappeared. The executioner fished about in the oil with a sieve, but there was no trace of Monkey, and the King called his guards to seize Tripitaka and the others. In great fear and sorrow, Tripitaka begged the King for time to honour the dead. He walked towards the cauldron and spoke respectfully to the soul of Monkey, but Pigsy came up and pushed him aside.

'Say this, Master – cursed ape, you have found the trouble that you sought, idiot, fool, we're well rid of you.' And so he continued, cursing and insulting, until Monkey rose up from the cauldron in anger, and shouted at him.

Bewildered, the court officials ran to the King, but the officer said, 'Fear not, it is only Monkey's ghost that troubles us.' Whereupon Monkey, still in a rage, ran up to the officer with his cudgel and began to beat him, saying, 'So if I'm a ghost, how does this feel?' All present were terrified and the three prisoners were released, but Monkey still demanded that Ram Strength take his turn in the cauldron. The third Immortal did not hesitate, and, flinging off his robe, he leapt into the boiling oil, where he began washing himself as if he were in his bath at home. Monkey perceived that he had a cold dragon within the pot and he interceded with the Dragon King of the Northern Ocean to remove the pest.

'Great sage,' said the Dragon King, 'this creature knows only a few miserable tricks that have nothing to do with the true Way of the Taoist.' Descending upon the cauldron in a magical whirlwind, the Dragon King took away the chilly dragon, and soon the Immortal began to struggle and writhe, but despite all his efforts he could not get out of the cauldron, and he was boiled alive. When the oil was cooled and strained, all that was found within it was the skeleton of a ram.

The King wept in despair, but Monkey went to him and said, 'Great King, see now that these creatures in whom you placed your trust were merely animals who were waiting for a chance to seize your power, when your authority should weaken. We four Buddhists have liberated you.'

The King dried his eyes and looked about him. 'You speak truth,' he said. He ordered a great banquet to be placed before the four travellers and all the officials and ladies of the court attended, praising Monkey as their saviour. The Buddhists were all released and given back their rights, and Monkey was praised and adored.

'Give due reverence to the Three Religions, which are indeed One,' he told the assembled company. 'Respect priests, respect Taoists and respect also human abilities. These hills and valleys will now be forever safe.' The King gave equal status to Taoism and Buddhism, and that decree was proclaimed throughout the land.

The travellers partook of the banquet and were then escorted by the King and members of the court beyond the city walls.

And so the four pilgrims resumed their quest. After braving many more adventures and travelling many thousands of leagues, they eventually brought the Buddhist scriptures to China.

Commentary

The story of Monkey King is the classic tale of how Buddhism came to China and asserted its superiority over the old Taoist practices. The above is a very small excerpt from a long saga. It was written down and embellished by Wu Ch'eng-en in the sixteenth century, based on much earlier material. Tripitaka was, in fact, a real person, Hsuan Tsang, who lived in the seventh century, and whose journey is well documented. The story of Monkey King has been extensively adapted for stage and screen.

THE INTEGRATION OF BUDDHISM

The arrival of Buddhism into China was no small event, and it caused much religious strife. This story is in some ways an attempt to reconcile Taoism and Buddhism, showing that Buddhism is superior to Taoism, but, paradoxically, that Taoism is its equal. A hint concerning this is given at the end of the 'Monkey King' tale, when the Dragon King of the Northern Ocean states that the Immortals in the story are not true Taoists. Buddhism as a religion is much more judgemental than Taoism. While on the face of it the story illustrates the triumph of Buddhism, in that the scriptures are obtained and brought back, the real hero is the unprincipled Trickster, Monkey, who has very little about him that is Buddhist. Monkey is shown up in a much better light than Tripitaka, for Monkey is fearless, while Tripitaka is often terrified and tearful. In addition, Monkey has a sense of humour and is endowed with considerable magical powers. We can see this story as a vital attempt to integrate forces that to some extent are inimical. At a very basic level it concerns instinct and intellect. These cannot be integrated by logic nor can they be in exact agreement, but they can work together for the same goals, as do Monkey and Tripitaka. The myth illustrates what may be hard to explain. The integration of these two religions is very basic to understanding China and its mythology.

THE FOUR PILGRIMS: FOUR FUNCTIONS OF CONSCIOUSNESS

The pilgrims may be seen as representing the four functions of consciousness, as defined by Jung. Jung taught that there are four mental functions, and that we all have one, two or possibly three of them working well, while the fourth is 'inferior', working unconsciously or in an undifferentiated fashion, and often to our detriment. Having all four functions working effectively is part of the process of individuation. These four functions he called Thinking, Feeling, Sensation and Intuition. Thinking and Feeling are a pair of opposites, and it is not possible to have them both fully conscious at the same time. Both of these are evaluative functions. Thinking operates through logical constructs, Feeling (which is not the same as emotion) judges on the basis of human bonds and interconnections. Intuition and Sensation are also opposites, both being perceptual. Intuition perceives the whole, and because of this it may appear to see around corners, although it misses details. Sensation relies on the evidence of the five senses.

The four pilgrims do not necessarily correspond exactly to the functions, although parallels can be drawn. It is tempting to see

Monkey as Intuition, Tripitaka as Thinking, Pigsy as Sensation and Sandy as Feeling. However, what is more to the point is that of the four, one is paramount in skill and action (Monkey), one supports (Tripitaka) but is sometimes ineffectual, and two are seldom useful and sometimes distinctly troublesome (as Pigsy and Sandy are when they appear to be mocking Monkey in the story given here). The human personality is built in this way: some parts function well, others not so well, and some are saboteurs. At another level, Monkey can be seen as human nature, which is capable of being redeemed, Sandy is frailty, which can be encouraged, Pigsy is the brute nature which can be repressed, and Tripitaka is the fine essence, which can attain immortality. Modern interpretations balk at the idea of 'suppression' and prefer to see Pigsy as a necessary energy, which proves useful and needs to be made more fully conscious. In addition, Tripitaka is often shown as rather pathetic, while Monkey is supreme. Another way of assigning the characters is that Monkey is the restless spirit of genius, Tripitaka the ordinary man, and Pigsy brute strength, while Sandy has been associated by some commentators with 'whole-heartedness'. Sandy does not feature much in this excerpt, but he may be seen as an unspoken, unifying principle. The horse ridden by Tripitaka may be man's animal nature. In a general sense the story of Monkey's travels is an allegory for the human passage through life, holding together the various forces within the personality and trying to balance and develop them.

THE BIRTH OF MONKEY

Monkey is initially a Stone Monkey who is born from a rock that becomes an egg. So Monkey comes from the earth herself, replete with instinctual wisdom and power. The sun, the moon and the winds acted upon this egg, so it was composed of Yin and Yang, and the forces of nature. As wind is readily linked to intellect, Monkey is a clever combination of the power of the earth and the spark of intelligence. As he emerges from his egg he acknowledges the Four Quarters. This is a powerful grounding process, affirming his 'earthiness'. It is also the basis for rituals which call on these quarters as guardians, for they represent the earthly state and are indicative of manifestation and completion in the world of matter. The Jade Emperor acknowledges that anything can happen in this cauldron of the material world, where basic matter is infused by spirit.

MONKEY'S ADVENTURES

Because Monkey has enterprise and initiative, he becomes king of the monkeys. He has the courage to go behind the veil of water. This means he looks behind appearances, and it is one of the things that gives him his strength. As water often symbolizes emotions, Monkey may be seen at once as willing to immerse himself in these, but also to progress beyond them. In so doing he grows as an individual. Although this is a waterfall, and thus not still enough to provide a reflection, water does have the facility to reflect back to us what we are. So we may stretch this analogy to cover that of going beyond the surface image, or behind the mask to the real self within. This is an obvious allegory for what goes on within the enterprising human being who takes on the challenges of life and has the courage to change. Monkey becomes king of all he surveys, but this is not enough, because he has not passed beyond the ordinary world. His is the spirit of the Seeker, and he becomes sad that he is bound to the 'mortal coil', so he goes off to seek immortality. Monkey then becomes guilty of 'hubris'; he begins to consider himself all powerful and even challenges the gods. This is a danger for all of us, as we evolve spiritually and as our mature personalities become powerful and integrated. To poor Monkey's credit, however, he acquits himself very well against all the pompous fools, clowns and bureaucrats of the Jade Emperor's court, and is only vanquished when something more meaningful comes along.

THE HAND OF THE BUDDHA

The episode where Monkey discovers that he cannot leave the palm of the Buddha, even by going to the ends of the universe, is a memorable one. This demonstrates that truth is inescapable, wherever you go. It is also a neat way of portraying infinity, which cannot be encompassed by the conscious mind. That the Buddha is of the very essence of creation is shown by the fact that his fingers and thumb turn into the five Chinese elements, which are the forces behind and within the manifest world. These imprison Monkey now, who was their master, and his fate is sealed by the sacred chant 'Om Mani Padme Hum'. Although the words are stamped over his prison, it is interesting to remember the importance of the chant in the changing of consciousness. The exact pronunciation of the sounds is very important, for sound has a vibration, and existence is composed of vibrations. Thus sound is potentially highly creative and basic to existence. This is paralleled in the biblical belief, 'In the beginning was the Word …' In this thinking, we have progressed beyond the alchemy and magical trigrams of Lao Tzu into something more pure and omnipresent. This, of course, may be the Buddhist view, though not shared by Taoists, many of whom were aware of ritual practices and the power of sound.

MONEY AS TRICKSTER

The Trickster motif appears in many stories and mythologies, and we briefly encountered it in the story of 'Yi the Archer' (Chapter 3). He is the first stage in the development of the myth of the Hero. Examples of the Trickster include such diverse figures as Brer Rabbit and Loki, in Norse mythology. In some ways the Trickster is related to the Intuitive function. The Trickster aids us by keeping fiction alive. This is not the same as delusion; rather, it keeps possibilities open, helping us to cope with stark reality. The Trickster is there to show that rules do not always have to be obeyed and that received wisdom is not all powerful. He shakes us awake and turns around our perceptions – by employing shock tactics. The desires of the Trickster decide his actions, and while he may appear unfeeling, Monkey in the story is an inspiration and a protective force to the other monkeys, all the while he is causing chaos in Heaven. In myth the Trickster is often shown in animal form (and Monkey is, after all, a monkey) but as the story evolves he becomes more human, in the same way that consciousness develops and matures.

The Trickster is a personification of the tricks that the unconscious mind plays on consciousness, in order to shake us out of our complacency. While the Trickster may seem cynical and destructive, he knows a thing or two and is part of the route to Wisdom. His tricks may be a kind of mirror-image of what is outwardly real. Like Hermes/Mercury in Greek and Roman myth, the Trickster represents movement within the psyche. As Hermes was able to pass in and out of the Underworld, so the Trickster moves between the conscious mind and the unconscious, enabling dynamic change to take place, not only crossing boundaries but disturbing them. Monkey is shown as being able to move between Heaven and Earth, but also into Underworld places inhabited by dragons, in passages not here retold.

Essentially the message of the Trickster is one of potential balance and completion. He may be (but is not always) associated with the inferior function in the psyche, which does not work smoothly, but trips us up because we are not aware of its perspectives, as we would be if we were whole. This inferior function inhabits the boundary area between the conscious mind and the unconscious. The Trickster is very much alive, and his ambivalence represents the vitality of truth, as opposed to the deadness of mere concept. So, while in the myth Monkey seems to be a champion of Buddhism (his cudgel perhaps indicative of the rigidity of doctrine), Monkey is also proof that doctrine has no meaning, for his very function is to transcend boundaries and bring transformation. He can shape-shift, becoming a gnat where appropriate, disguising himself as a Taoist monk and even as a tin tack. His companions are not immune to his trickery, and poor Tripitaka dies a thousand deaths as a result of his antics. Culturally, it is the ideas that shock conventional mores which give the impetus for change, and while the shocking element may not be adopted wholesale, it is the agent for change. Within the personality a similar dynamic is at work, where impulses emerge within us that may shake us, but are most fruitfully regarded as liberating forces that may not be taken on wholesale, but need to be integrated, for growth.

THE THREE IMMORTALS

Deer Strength, Ram Strength and Tiger Strength are clearly a reference to earlier, shamanistic beliefs, where animals are regarded as a source of power, and power animals are adopted by those who journey between the worlds. The implication is that Taoism is merely shamanism or similar in disguise. However this is ambiguous, for Monkey, Pigsy and Sandy are all animals too!

CART SLOW

The name of the country where the main events take place is Cart Slow. This implies a place that is behind the times, where ancient practices are still regarded as supreme. The Taoists are made into figures of fun, drinking urine in their search for immortality. However, it is revealed at the end of the tale that the three Immortals were not even Taoists, but animals conspiring to take over the kingdom. Thus Buddhism, in the ironical shape of Monkey, is shown to save humanity from its lower, 'animal' nature.

THE THREE ORDEALS

The three Immortals (ordeals) proclaim that they can be beheaded, gutted and boiled in oil, but still survive. Again we have a relic of shamanism, for dismemberment and reforging in a cauldron was a metaphor for transformation. Such ordeals are often experienced in dream form as part of the initiation process. Indeed, there are verified accounts of initiates undergoing seemingly impossible ordeals on the way to becoming fully fledged shamans.

12

Tales of Dragons

The Dragon King's Daughter

Having passed his examinations, a young man called Liu was returning home from the capital when he saw a young shepherdess. She was the loveliest woman Liu had ever seen, but she was weeping bitterly, the tears coursing down her cheeks. Deeply moved, Liu got down from his horse and went over to her, asking her why she was crying.

'I am married to the god of the Jing river, whom I do not love,' she told him through her sobs. 'He is cruel to me, but I am too far away from my father for him to help me. He is the Dragon King of Lake Dongting, and would help me if he could, but here I am alone and with not a friend in the world.'

'Tell me what I can do to help you, fair maiden,' pleaded Liu, who was touched by her story.

The girl looked at him. 'You will need to be of stout heart,' she said. 'Go to the tangerine tree by the lake, tie your sash on it and knock three times. Someone will come to lead you to my father.' She took a letter for him to give to the Dragon King, and as he left she called out, 'I hope we shall meet again when you return to Dongting.' But when he turned round to wave goodbye, the young woman was gone.

Liu went to the lake and did as she had told him, whereupon a man rose from the waves and enquired about his mission. He placed a blindfold over Liu's eyes and led him to a place where a great coldness flowed over him, but soon the blindfold was removed and he opened his eyes to find himself in a magnificent palace, surrounded by gold and jewels. Before him, on a huge throne, sat the mighty Dragon King.

Liu handed him the letter, and on reading it enormous tears ran down his great cheeks. He instructed the letter to be taken to the chambers of the Queen, whereupon a great wailing was heard from the women's quarters.

'Tell them to be quiet,' said the King, 'or Chiantang will get upset.'

'Who is Chiantang?' asked Liu, in surprise.

'He is my brother,' replied the Dragon King. 'Once he too was Dragon King of his own lake, but his temper was too unpredictable and the gods gave him into my keeping, to vouch for his good behaviour. He dearly loves his niece and this news would immediately rouse him to vengeance.'

Just as he finished speaking the chamber was filled with a great noise and through it rushed a huge red dragon. Liu fell down in fear, but as quickly as he had appeared, he was gone again.

The Dragon King helped Liu to get up. 'I do apologize for my brother,' he said. 'That was Chiantang who just came by. Please do not worry, but enjoy this banquet I have ordered to be spread for you.'

Honoured, Liu recovered his composure and sat eating, drinking and discussing his travels with the Dragon King. While they were eating, the Queen and her ladies came in, and to his amazement Liu saw that the daughter of the Dragon King was there amongst them! She thanked Liu for his help, while her father embraced her and begged her forgiveness. Soon an elegant young man entered the room and joined them. He was introduced to Liu as Chiantang. In response to his brother's questions, Chiantang recounted how he had vanquished the army of the god of the Jing River, and had won the approval of the High Gods for his actions.

'And what of Jing himself?' asked Liu, intrigued.

'I ate him,' replied Chiantang, and they all continued with the meal.

The days continued with feasting and celebration, all in honour of Liu, and in due course Chiantang took him aside and suggested to him that he marry his niece, with whom Liu was obviously very much in love. But Chiantang had enjoyed several glasses of rice wine and

Liu was afraid that, when sober, the fearsome dragon might change his mind. So he talked the Dragon King out of his idea and left the next day, with his arms full of gifts, yet his heart was heavy.

Liu soon married a local girl, for he reasoned that he could not forever yearn after the Dragon Princess. But his wife fell sick and died of the fever, and when he remarried the same thing happened to his second wife. Lonely and bereft, Liu married for a third time, to a girl from foreign parts, who bore a son for him. Strange and wonderful to tell, his third wife began to look more and more like the lost love of his youth, the Dragon Princess, and after the birth of their second son she revealed that she was, in fact, this very person. She had been deeply disappointed when Liu had turned down her uncle's suggestion. She had been watching him and when his second wife had died she had seized her opportunity to marry him.

After this they lived in great happiness, raising a large family together and paying frequent visits to the court of the Dragon King. When Liu became older, they took up residence there with the Immortals, and were never again seen in the ordinary world of men.

The Dragon's Pearl

Once a mother and her son lived beside the River Min, eking out a meagre living. The boy worked long hours cutting grass to feed the animals, to support his ailing mother, but they barely survived. As the year advanced and the weather became dryer, he was forced to venture further and further afield to find any crop. On one especially hot day he had travelled many miles, all to no avail, and was about to return home, empty handed and exhausted, when he spied a patch of tall, lush grass. He recovered his energy at this fortunate discovery, cut the grass and went home very happy.

The next day he returned, hoping for similar luck, but to his surprise the very same patch had grown again. This happened day after day, until the son and his mother were much better off. The only drawback was that the boy had to travel so far each day to get the grass.

He made a plan to move the grass closer to home, and spent the whole of a long, hot day digging up the turf and carrying it back to his own land. In so doing he found a wonderful pearl, which he gave

Figure 12.1 *The rising celestrial dragon with the pearl representing concentrated human cosmic energy. Detail from Mandarin robe, 1796–1820, Ch'ing dynasty.*

to his mother in excitement. For safety she hid it in the bottom of a rice jar, and the exhausted boy slept deeply.

The next morning he awoke full of enthusiasm to harvest the grass nearer home, but to his dismay the turf was brown and bare. Just as he was about to lose himself in lamentation, he and his mother noticed that the rice jar, which had been almost empty, was now brimming over with white, shiny rice. Then they knew that this was a magic pearl. They placed it in their money box, and the next morning it was full to overflowing with sparkling coins.

Mother and son were now very wealthy and they took pride in being good to the villagers who had helped them when times were hard. However, there were those who grew curious as to the source of their good fortune, and soon many people knew about the wonderful pearl. One day a crowd of the less kindly people from the village came and surrounded the boy, demanding that the magic pearl be shared. Not knowing what to do the boy put the pearl in his mouth and swallowed it.

Immediately he was consumed by a fiery thirst that he could not slake. He drunk the well dry as a bone and then started to drink from the river, which disappeared into his mouth, as the terrified villagers watched him. As the last of the River Min slid down his throat, there was a crash of thunder, dark clouds gathered and a huge storm broke over the village. As for the boy, he sprouted horns, grew scales and a long, lashing tail. Bigger and bigger he grew before the eyes of his devastated mother, who now understood that the pearl must have belonged to the River Dragon. Every water dragon possessed a pearl which he guarded as his greatest treasure – and now her son was turning into a dragon. As the water fell in torrents the bed of the river began to fill up and the dragon boy slid further and further along the mud and down into the growing stream. His poor mother tried frantically to hold on to his rough legs, but he could not stay. Thrashing and twisting, he looked at her for one last time, as he vanished beneath the waves for ever. And to this very day the banks of the River Min are called the Looking Back at Mother banks, in memory of the hapless boy and his priceless dragon pearl.

Commentary

The above are two examples of many folk tales that involve dragons.

DRAGONS

In the mythology of the West, dragons are usually represented as fearsome and destructive. Being connected to snakes and 'worms', they have links with the underground, usually inhabiting dark caves. These associations hark back to much earlier pagan cultures in which the feminine was held in greater esteem. The earth and the snake are linked with the Mother Goddess who became demonized as patriarchy gained a hold. This process is immortalized in such tales as that of the Sumerian god Marduk, who slew his ancestor Tiamat, the dragon, from whose body the world was made. The ancient idea that dragons are associated with the earth is currently gaining new credibility in the East. Even in the West 'dragon power', seen, for example, in ley lines, is considered positive by those who believe in it.

Chinese mythology, while extremely patriarchal in the way it is currently perceived, has always held a very different view of dragons to that of the West. Although these creatures are indeed fearsome, in the East they are essentially forces for good. Within the mythology of China there are examples of evil dragons being fought against by the 'hero' but these monsters are from foreign parts, and symbolize the national paranoid view of the cultural 'other'. Ancient Chinese bronze castes, made before the invention of writing, are decorated with these creatures. Each location has its dragon, and these would be approached as one would approach a human ruler, regarding them as fair but stern. The dragon is also a symbol of power and is found embroidered on royal robes.

Dragons feature in the tale of 'Monkey King' (Chapter 11), as great beings in the sky who control the weather. More specifically, one quarter of the heavens is called the Palace of the Green Dragon, connected to the stars that, to Chinese astronomers, form the constellation of the Dragon. The appearance of this group of stars is a harbinger of the rainy season, for even heavenly dragons are associated with water. On earth, each body of water has its own dragon, and the larger the expanse the greater the power of the Dragon Lord. The local dragon may be petitioned for favours, and the weather was often the subject for these requests.

In Chinese mythology, dragons pull the chariot of the Lady Queen of the West, Hsi Wang Mu, that of the Sun, and other deities. Various other dragons have been described, such as the Hidden Treasures Dragon who guards all such hoards, the Spirit Dragon who specifically produces rain, and the Heavenly Dragon who guards the realms of the gods. The true Chinese dragon, however, in contrast to Western adaptations, has fins rather than wings. The ability to disgorge pearls is frequently encountered, and these are often shown coming from a dragon's mouth and encircled by flames. The dragon is regarded as the monarch over all creatures with scales, such as fish and reptiles. When it wishes it can become invisible. For half the year it lives in its patch of water, but in the spring, when the dragon constellation rises to the meridian, it ascends into the sky. The Chinese word for dragon is *lung* and because this is the same sounding word as for 'deaf', dragons have been regarded as not being able to hear, although this is not borne out by accounts in legends.

As with so many elements of Chinese thought and mythology, with the advent of Buddhism the dragon became absorbed into the mythology and art of the new religion, although it did not originate with them.

The number nine, the symbolism of which is discussed in the commentary after 'Yu and the Floodwaters' (Chapter 4), features in dragon lore. The dragon is said to be composed of nine creatures, having the head of a camel, the horns of a deer, the eyes of a rabbit, the ears of a cow, the neck of a snake, the belly of a frog, the scales of a fish, the claws of a hawk and the paws of a tiger. To ancient shamanic cultures this would have conveyed much about the magical strength of the dragon, drawing on the powers of all these creatures. In Beijing there is a famous screen, called the Nine Dragon Screen, depicting the nine different species of dragon in their natural place, such as on the roof of a temple, the hilt of a sword, etc. Similar screens can be found all over China, and the Beijing design has been extensively reproduced.

The four directions of the compass have been represented since at least as early as the second century bce by four animals: the White Tiger of the West, the Black Tortoise of the North, the Red Bird of the South and the Green Dragon of the East. For the Chinese, the expanse of water that is the Pacific lies to the east. It is also the home of the sunrise. The Dragon is also the fifth animal of the Chinese zodiac (see Chapter 15). The four heavenly creatures have no connection with the 12 animals of the Zodiac, which are a much later addition, evolving no earlier than 600 CE. The supposed attributes of individuals born during the Year of the Dragon include strength and wisdom, although they are powerful enemies, which concurs with the image of the dragon.

Psychologically the image of the dragon has a significance that spans cultural divides. Because it generally inhabits the underground or the depths of a lake, it has obvious links with the unconscious mind. Whether the dragon is seen as positive or negative has interesting implications in terms of the cultural attitude towards inward transformation. The hero, in conflict with the dragon, is the ego threatened by the powers of the unconscious, or the light of consciousness that can be swallowed by the earth and the heaviness of matter. Eastern dragons, with their wings (although, as we have seen, these may be fins) and also their crowns, indicate the attitude of the Chinese, for whom the transformation of the unconscious into creativity was considered an important life's work. Specifically they symbolize the power of intuition, which has creatively changed the relationship between the ego and natural forces. Because dragons are associated with specific elements, psychologically they may be an indication that one of the functions is operating in an inferior fashion and needs to be transformed (see the commentary following the tale of 'Monkey King' in Chapter 11 for an explanation of the four functions of consciousness). In the case of Chinese dragons, which are mostly aquatic, we may speculate that the Feeling function is culturally the inferior one. This is borne out by the traditional view that the West is concerned with Love, the East with Wisdom, and indeed Chinese systems and customs are cerebral and complex. The representation of the dragon as 'good', however, is encouraging for the pursuit of balance. Because the dragon appears as a composite animal, it represents many combined elements within the psyche that may need to be differentiated and consciously related to each other. These essences may be seen in a variety of ways. One way of looking at them is shamanically: the dragon could be a composite of power animals or instinctual forces that, if heeded, could be powerful allies indeed. The dragon is therefore a numinous figure, which may be seen as symbolizing an inner creative process.

Dragons in the two myths come in a variety of guises. In the first one we see the glamour of the Dragon Princess, which draws Liu into the potentially transforming situation, also the lordly persona of her father and the ferocious aspect of her uncle. All of these may be taken as different aspects of the same process. In the second tale all we see of the dragon is its pearl with its potential rewards, which are abused and therefore become ultimately destructive. Dragon gifts are meant for more than the mere feeding of the physical body.

THE HERO'S ATTITUDE

The two folk tales show different approaches to fortune on the part of the hero. Liu's attitude is extremely respectful and wary. He is delighted with the honours shown to him, but does not presume upon his good fortune. He is rewarded by the hand of the Dragon Princess, only after essentially avoiding the honour and trying to live without it. One cannot resist wondering whether the two prior marriages were indeed some kind of test of how enduring his feelings towards the princess really were. Would his wives have died if he had really been devoted to them? When he does marry the Dragon Princess, he does not at once recognize her, indicating that the numinous is not always obvious.

In contrast the poor boy in the second tale has no such respect or awareness. Ignorance is no protection when he unknowingly swallows the dragon's pearl – nor can his previous kindness help him. Although he and his mother have given of their worldly goods, that is not enough. To deserve the gifts of the dragon one must be wise as well as generous. The dragon stands outside conventional morality, and demands growth of some description. Whereas Liu is humble in the face of the numinous and has some awareness of what he is dealing with, the poor boy and his mother do not. The end of the tale of 'The Dragon's Pearl' is harsh, and indicates the unsentimental attitude sometimes conveyed in Chinese myths. The 'Looking Back at Mother' banks are a monument not so much to filial and maternal devotion as to foolishness. The message of these stories is that we should approach the numinous and the riches of the unconscious with respect. Liu receives his award as he matures, and eventually disappears from the mortal world altogether, his transformation complete.

THE THEME OF TRANSFORMATION

In both the myths, transformations take place by means of the dragons. In the case of Liu we may assume that an expansion of consciousness takes place. The Dragon Princess is an 'anima' figure, signifying his contra-sexual self. When he 'marries' her he has access to unconscious elements within himself and he gradually becomes complete. This takes place after struggle and bravery. His first challenge was to brave the realms of the Dragon King in order to save the princess. The second was to sustain the presence of the mighty Chiantang, in restraint and wisdom, while the third was to guard within his heart his love for the princess. Apart from the initial courageous encounter with the numinous forces, by the banks of the lake and the tangerine tree, he achieves such qualities as respect, restraint and a balanced attitude. The entire encounter seems like a test to see how he handles himself in the god-like realms.

No such restraint or even common sense influences the behaviour of the peasant boy, who, when under threat by the villagers, swallows the pearl, and takes into himself all its magical power. The human frame cannot sustain the dragon power, so he undergoes an agonizing, hideous transformation, not, we assume, into a dragon of celestial character, but into a slimy, scaly creature, as if his lower, unconscious essence overtakes him entirely. One imagines the Dragon King who owns the pearl watching the process. However, the boy does himself become a dragon, in whatever guise, and one may like to imagine that the old dragon takes him under his wing so that he, too, may eventually be transformed.

THE PEARL

The pearl signifies the treasure at the heart, the enduring and incorruptible essence that remains when the work of life is complete. The oyster makes the pearl as a protection from irritation within its shell demonstrating that suffering can be a refining and creative process. The appearance of the pearl being white, like the moon, may indicate that it is associated with the anima. In fact, Aphrodite, the Greek goddess of love, was depicted as rising from a shell.

The pearl in the second story is a parallel with the Dragon Princess of the first. The pearl is the precious essence that can create and create endlessly, but must be treated with respect. The Dragon Princess has dangerous relations and so must be approached slowly and reverently. If honoured, however, she will be helpful and fruitful. It is only in his marriage with her that Liu has children. Fruitfulness is also presaged by the tangerine tree, where Liu has to meet the otherworldly being.

TIME AND AWARENESS IN THE STORY OF THE DRAGON PRINCESS

In common with Western tales of sojourn in the Otherworld, time seems to have a different quality in the realm of the dragon gods. Linear attitudes to time do not apply in unconscious or magical realms. Thus the vengeance of Chiantang and the return of the princess are accomplished 'in a twinkling'. Mystics claim that time is a construct of the rational, restricted mind and that cosmic consciousness is outside time. Hints are thus given that the events take place outside the 'normal' time frame, in the realm of an expanded awareness. This is also hinted at in the second story by the grass that grows to full height overnight, in defiance of natural cycles. At the start of the tale we are told that Liu has 'passed his examinations' indicating that he has mastered earthly knowledge. Eventually Liu leaves the world of men and goes to live in that of the gods, indicating that he has acquired insight beyond wisdom and now exists in a state of cosmic consciousness.

13

The Willow Pattern

There was once a powerful mandarin, who lived in a beautiful two-storey mansion. However, he was old, and quite lonely. His wife had recently died and he was becoming too infirm to minister his estates adequately. So he employed a secretary to help him in the task, and lived his life essentially apart from the world.

The mandarin had a beautiful daughter, but he was so blind to all but his own selfish concerns that he failed to notice that she and his new secretary were falling in love. They began to meet in secret, for they knew that her father would not approve of their liaison. Night after night they met in the shadows of the willow trees that grew in the garden, until one bright evening when the moon rode high they were spotted by one of the servants. Eager to curry favour with his master, the servant ran to the mandarin and told what he had seen.

In a mighty rage the mandarin summoned his guards and ordered them to seize the secretary. When the young man was dragged before him the mandarin demanded to know what was happening, and the secretary, never wishing to be anything but honest about his love, bravely asked for the hand of the mandarin's daughter in marriage.

This further enraged the lord, and he banished the secretary with no money and no food, taking only the clothes that were on his back. He locked his weeping daughter in her room. Then he ordered that a high wall be built around the house, its gardens and surrounding willows, so that it would be forever hidden and the girl unable to escape. Meanwhile another man sought the hand of the mandarin's daughter. She would have nothing to do with him, and spent her time sitting at the window, gazing out at the willow trees under which she and her lover had spent so many blissful moments. She did not know what had become of him, but she hoped against hope that he was waiting for her, somewhere beyond the harsh walls that surrounded her, and that one day he would rescue her and they would be reunited.

One day the rich suitor was being entertained by her father. This man had brought a casket of fine jewels which he laid before the mandarin.

'This and more shall be yours', said the suitor, 'if you will give me your daughter to wife.'

The mandarin looked at the shining jewels with covetous eyes. 'Alas,' he said, 'the girl is so stubborn. Since I banished my secretary she has not come out of her room. She had a silly crush on him and I can do nothing with her.'

'I am sure she can be persuaded,' said the suitor, and they spoke at length about the matter, and about their finances, as the shadows grew long beneath the willow trees. No one noticed a rope snake over the wall, in the twilight, or saw the daughter of the mandarin as she slipped out, across the darkening lawns and into the arms of her lover. Soon they were away, galloping off into the night, their horses' hoof-beats sounding like thunder on the bridge. Behind them in the distance there were loud shouts while lanterns waved crazily as her father set off in belated, futile pursuit. Meanwhile, their saddlebags jangling with the jewels the audacious young man had stolen from under the drunken noses of her father and the suitor, the girl laughed with relief that she was now free.

The couple made their way to a humble cottage, where they were safe, and enjoyed a few days of bliss while they planned the next stage of their journey, which was to escape on the river by boat. But they delayed too long. One night there was a pounding on the cottage door and there stood her father's armed men. They seized the girl's lover, and the suitor had him executed for the theft of the jewels. Then the horrified girl, knowing that her father intended to make her marry this monstrous man, took her own life.

But that is not the end of the story for, in death, the lovers were reunited, flying above in the shape of two cranes that forever soar in the skies over the lake.

Commentary

The Tale of the Willow Pattern is well known as being a Western fabrication and having no true place in Chinese mythology. It is included here because it seems, nevertheless, to express something quintessentially Chinese, which is probably why it captured popular Western imagination at the time. The pattern was created in 1780 for Thomas Turner's porcelain factory in Caughley by Thomas Minton, and the story was later constructed in order to boost sales of the crockery.

THE CRANES

The symbolism of cranes is explored in the commentary on the myth of 'Yi the Archer' (Chapter 3). They are well known as being connected with death and the passage of the soul. In general, birds symbolize the connection between the material and spiritual realms. Images of the crane were placed on coffins, as they were purported to transport the departed soul to paradise. The crane was especially important to the Chinese, being regarded as sovereign over the other birds. A single feather from a bird is believed to carry the essence of the entire bird. Such ideas are common in magical and shamanistic practice. Cranes were believed to live for over 600 years, after which they stopped eating. In the seventh century crane feathers were popularly used in the uniforms of the royal guards and because of this cranes were hunted almost to the point of extinction. The incorporation of the crane into this tale is therefore extremely appropriate in connection with Chinese mythology.

THE BRIDGE

The bridge symbolizes transition from one state to another, in this case from life to death. Similarly it forms a link between the conscious and the unconscious mind. The bridge offers a way to pass over the water, which may be seen as the 'feeling' realm. However, the lovers cannot cross over the larger stretch of water, for they cannot find a boat. This may be seen as their inability to go beyond the throes of passion and form a deeper relationship. Another way of looking at it is that they are unable to make conscious what is happening and so become lost. The tale can be taken as one of transformation and transcendence (into the immortal shape of the crane) but also as a warning of what happens if we cannot transform, for then a part of us dies.

THE WILLOW TREE

The tree is an important symbol. According to many models, the cosmos is conceived as structured around the world tree, which has its roots in the Lower World, its trunk in the Middle World, and its branches in the Upper World. These three worlds constitute the home of different sorts of spirits and offer different experiences to the ascending shaman. On a practical level, trees are necessary to our ecology, being the 'lungs' of the planet.

The willow is especially important to the Chinese, being associated with the goddess of compassion, Kuan Yin. Kuan means 'earth', and Yin, as we know, relates to the force of the feminine. She sprinkles the waters of life with a willow branch and is often shown riding a dolphin. She is sometimes featured in the myth of Monkey King, helping the pilgrims with her special magic. Other Chinese associations with the willow include many so-called 'feminine' attributes, such as grace, charm, artistic ability and meekness. Taoists regard it as representing strength in weakness, for it bends before the storm but does not break, whereas mightier trees such as the oak stand firm and are often broken. Because the willow seeks water in this quest, it is associated especially with the moon (ruler of the tides). Thus the willow is linked to the feeling side, to the fluctuating emotions which the moon's phases represent, and to intuition. In Europe the willow is associated with death, and also with unrequited love. It is thought to be 'weeping', because of the trailing strands formed by its leaves.

Figure 13.1 Kuan Yin

Those who chose the willow for this pattern, and to feature in the story, must have known about the willow associations, or been very much in tune with time-honoured willow meanings.

14

The Herdsman and the Weaver Girl

Aeons ago, in the mists of the past, a little weaver girl spun and sewed in the Palace of the Gods, making wonderful clothes in a myriad of shimmering, complex patterns. The High God loved her dearly and was delighted with her work, but he was worried that she laboured too hard. He decided to send her down to Earth and chose for her a husband, a herdsman called Chen-Li.

Chen-Li lived with his two brothers on a farm beside a great river. The brothers had inherited the farm from their parents but because Chen-Li was the youngest he only received an ox, along with the most infertile piece of land. But he was good-humoured and hard-working, which is why the High God had selected him for his weaver girl.

One evening Chen-Li sat lonely and tired, watching the sun go down. His ox was beside him, gently munching the grass.

'If only I had a wife to share my life with, then it would all seem worthwhile,' said Chen-Li to himself. To his amazement the ox replied to him.

'Do not be so sad, master' said the beast. 'I am the Ox Star sent to earth to help humans, and I have a message from the gods for you. If you go upstream you will find a beautiful, clear pool shaded by rushes and willows. The Heavenly Maidens go there to bathe each day and if you were to steal the clothes of one of them she would have to remain here on earth and, according to tradition, she would be your wife.'

Chen-Li could not wait for the following day, and when he had completed his work he stole upstream. Sure enough, there was the wonderful pool, filled with the most beautiful girls he had ever seen. He bounded from the bushes and stole a set of clothes. The girls leapt from the pool, snatched their clothes and soared upwards, leaving only one – the little weaver girl, whose garments Chen-Li held in his trembling hands. She looked shyly at Chen-Li and said:

'Sir, if you would kindly give me back my clothes I will return with you and be your wife.'

Chen-Li was overjoyed and led her back to the farm. They were married and spent many blissful years together, during which they had two children and the weaver girl forgot all about Heaven. But Heaven had not forgotten her and eventually the High God decided he could no longer do without his weaver girl and her fine fabrics. One day he sent soldiers down to escort her home. She begged and pleaded but the soldiers took her anyway. All poor Chen-Li could do was to look on helplessly, holding his two children, as the magical warriors carried her off.

His old ox saw his sorrow and told him not to worry. 'Soon I will die and return to my celestial home,' said the animal. 'You must skin me and wrap yourself in my hide. Then you will be able to follow your wife.' Instantly, the ox died. Chen-Li skinned it and wrapped around himself and his two children. Immediately they were airborne and following the trail of the weaver girl.

From his throne the High God saw all this and was much displeased. He cast down his white scarf, which turned into a fiery torrent, separating the lovers completely. Try as they might, neither could cross the shimmering river, for its heat sucked away their life. Defeated, the desolate Chen-Li returned home, but the High God was still watching. Seeing how truly the lovers missed each other he relented and passed a decree. On the seventh day of the seventh month all the magpies in the world would fly up to heaven and make a bridge so that the weaver girl and Chen-Li could be together, albeit briefly. Whenever they met, the weaver girl wept and her tears fell to earth as rain. All the women on earth also mourned, saying 'Our sister weeps once more.'

Chen-Li and the weaver girl spent so much time in the sky that they turned into stars. The weaver girl is Vega, the fiery stream is the Milky Way and on the other side Chen-Li is Aquila, with two small stars beside it, which are the couple's children. On the seventh day of the seventh month the stars are mysteriously united, giving hope to separated lovers all over the world.

Commentary

This myth was commemorated at the Qixi festival and is still celebrated in Japan as Tanabata. This takes place in July or August. Wishes are written on pieces of paper and hung on bamboo. They may also be set afloat in bamboo boats and burned the next day. Such celebrations bring a little magic into life and are a reminder that the cycles of heaven continue and that all changes, bringing hope of better times.

THE CLOTHES OF THE WEAVER GIRL

The clothes element of the story echoes such tales as that of the Selkie, where a hunter steals the skin of a beautiful seal woman and so she stays behind to be his wife. Taking the clothes, or the skin, deprives the divine or magical being of its connection to its source – temporarily. Such stories are usually shadowed by tragedy, because human is seeking to mate with the divine or mythical, and the bliss that is promised can never last. The wondrous must be appreciated for what it is – something to bring light and inspiration, but never to be possessed.

A LOVER FROM ANOTHER WORLD

Chen-Li has the gift of a celestial partner but he makes the mistake of allowing his whole existence to be consumed by her. Psychologically, this relates to the seductive contra-sexual part of the psyche – the animus or anima – which has such a powerful glamour, and who appears to Chen-Li in the form of his weaver girl. In ordinary life the enchantment of the anima may be projected onto a physical person, but while the relationship takes place with the anima, rather than the true human being, loss is bound to follow. Often a person who embodies the anima/animus may leave the relationship because they sense that there is no real connection. The other party, however, is aware only of having lost their heart's desire and can imagine no other fulfilment. This can leach the life energy and lead to loneliness and alienation, as Chen-Li spends his life gazing across the fiery river, yearning for his lost love. The lesson is to appreciate the anima/animus as it truly is – one's own soul, yearning to be complete. This is something that can only happen internally through a spiritual or creative quest. If the anima/animus can be experienced as inspiration rather than obsession, the result will be productive. The possibility of this is also present in the myth, showing a positive side in the shape of the couple's children.

15

....

The Chinese Zodiac

Twelve signs

There are 12 Chinese signs, just as there are 12 western ones, but instead of each sign spanning one month, the Chinese Zodiac Signs cover an entire year. Each year is named after an animal, and that animal epitomizes the character of the person born within the 12 months. The years alternate Yang and Yin, starting with Yang Rat, then Yin Ox, and so on. Because Chinese New Year is variable, starting on the second New Moon after the Midwinter Solstice, the table below shows which year you fall within if you were born in January or February. Chinese astrology is very complex, and the motion of the Moon is extremely important. Based on the phases of the Moon, each month lasts for 29 or 30 days, and is divided into two fortnights. There are ten days in the week and each day is divided into 12 segments of two hours each. Instead of the Western grouping into decades, the years are counted in cycles of 12, and the days organized into a complex cycle of number combinations. These include ten Heavenly Stems and Twelve Earthly Branches. These cycles of ten and 12 interweave and form the basis for further interpretations which are outside our scope here.

The legend of the naming of the years

Originally the Chinese years were numbered, just like the days. At some point this changed and they were given the exotic animal names that make them so memorable. The 'zo' of 'zodiac' means animal. However, in contrast to the figures of the Western zodiac, which are named after constellations, the Chinese zodiac has no such correlation. These 12 animals are regarded by some scholars as a fairly recent invention, historically speaking, at least in the form used currently. One theory is that they originally represented 12 ritual monthly or yearly sacrifices, but that is not substantiated (and it is hard to imagine how anyone could sacrifice a dragon). The 12 animals are also associated with the 12 two-hour periods that occur within the day.

Legend has it that the Buddha, on planning to leave this world, decided to invite all the animals to feast with him. He sent out invitations to all creatures, but of only 12 turned up. Reliable Ox led the way, but at the last moment the opportunistic Rat scampered along Ox's back and arrived first of all on the doorstep of the Buddha. The Buddha rewarded every one of them for their obedience and loyalty by naming a year after each of them, in the sequence in which they had turned up. The 12 animals are, in order: Rat, Ox, Tiger, Rabbit, Dragon, Snake, Horse, Sheep, Monkey, Rooster, Dog and Pig. These names are translated from the Chinese, and do vary. Goat may be substituted for Sheep, Buffalo or Cow for Ox, and Hare for Rabbit, for example. However, Westerners occasionally refer to the Year of the Rabbit as the Year of the Cat, and that is not authentic. Rabbits and Hares have long been associated with the Spring Equinox, and in the Chinese calendar the Spring Equinox always falls in the Rabbit month. This does not apply to the Cat and there are in fact at least two myths to account for the feline's absence. The Cat was indeed supposed to have come to the Buddha's to celebrate, but naughty Rat did not pass on the message, and Cat stayed curled up asleep, missing all the fun. Another story holds that Rat did tell Cat about the party, but Cat simply preferred to doze. In a third version, the Cat was excluded because it had caught a mouse.

In other versions of the legend the Jade Emperor summons the animals and sometimes the event is a race, rather than a banquet. Whatever the occasion, the animals get up to all sorts of trickery along the way. We have seen how Rat got in first. Snake was also sneaky. It hid on Horse's hoof in order to cross a river. On reaching the far bank it spooked Horse, and so beat it in the contest. Dragon, however, proved to be honourable and altruistic. Powerful, magical and gifted with the ability to fly, it could have won, hands down, but it stopped to help some villagers who were caught in a flood. Other versions recount how Dragon helped Rabbit over the torrent, and yet another version has the opposite angle – Dragon lingered to create rain for parched farmland.

The history of the zodiac

The history of the birth of the Chinese zodiac is hard to establish. The animals were popular in the T'ang dynasty, appearing on pottery dating from the seventh century CE, but they were also to some extent evident during the turbulent Warring States Period in the fifth century BCE. Some say that the animals were brought to China along the Silk Road – the same central Asian trade route that brought the Buddhist belief from India to China. Scholars do not agree on this, and some argue that the animals predate Buddhism and are rooted in very ancient Chinese astrology that was based on the 12-year cycle of the planet Jupiter. Still others assert that nomadic tribes from ancient China compiled a calendar based on animals they used to hunt and herd.

Confucianism and the zodiac

The Confucian model of a hierarchical society fits in well with the concept that every animal has its place in the scheme of things, and in society. Confucian beliefs persist in modern China, alongside use of the zodiac. Births increased in the Dragon years 1988 and 2000 – the Dragon is considered to be the luckiest of the animals.

THE ELEMENTS AND THE ANIMALS

In Chinese astrology there are five elements, Earth, Fire, Wood, Water and Metal. These have different characteristics, explained in Chapter 4. The Chinese cycle consists of 60 years, as each of the animals comes under the direction of every element in turn, and the element modifies and overlays the animal personality. The following table gives the start date of the years, the element and animal.

1936	24 January	Fire	Rat
1937	11 February	Fire	Ox
1938	31 January	Earth	Tiger

1939	19 February	Earth	Rabbit
1940	8 February	Metal	Dragon
1941	27 January	Metal	Snake
1942	15 February	Water	Horse
1943	5 February	Water	Sheep
1944	25 January	Wood	Monkey
1945	13 February	Wood	Rooster
1946	2 February	Fire	Dog
1947	22 January	Fire	Pig
1948	10 February	Earth	Rat
1949	29 January	Earth	Ox
1950	17 February	Metal	Tiger
1951	6 February	Metal	Rabbit
1952	27 January	Water	Dragon
1953	14 February	Water	Snake
1954	3 February	Wood	Horse
1955	24 January	Wood	Sheep
1956	12 February	Fire	Monkey
1957	31 January	Fire	Rooster
1958	18 February	Earth	Dog
1959	8 February	Earth	Pig
1960	28 January	Metal	Rat
1961	15 February	Metal	Ox
1962	5 February	Water	Tiger
1963	25 January	Water	Rabbit
1964	13 February	Wood	Dragon
1965	2 February	Wood	Snake
1966	21 January	Fire	Horse
1967	9 February	Fire	Sheep
1968	30 January	Earth	Monkey

1969	17 February	Earth	Rooster
1970	6 February	Metal	Dog
1971	27 January	Metal	Pig
1972	16 January	Water	Rat
1973	3 February	Water	Ox
1974	23 January	Wood	Tiger
1975	11 February	Wood	Rabbit
1976	31 January	Fire	Dragon
1977	18 February	Fire	Snake
1978	7 February	Earth	Horse
1979	28 January	Earth	Sheep
1980	16 February	Metal	Monkey
1981	5 February	Metal	Rooster
1982	25 January	Water	Dog
1983	13 February	Water	Pig
1984	2 February	Wood	Rat
1985	20 February	Wood	Ox
1986	9 February	Fire	Tiger
1987	29 January	Fire	Rabbit
1990	27 January	Metal	Horse
1991	15 February	Metal	Sheep
1992	4 February	Water	Monkey
1993	23 January	Water	Rooster
1994	10 February	Wood	Dog
1995	31 January	Wood	Pig
1996	19 February	Fire	Rat
1997	8 February	Fire	Ox
1998	28 January	Earth	Tiger
1999	16 February	Earth	Rabbit
2000	5 February	Metal	Dragon

2001	24 January	Metal	Snake
2002	12 February	Water	Horse
2003	1 February	Water	Sheep
2004	22 January	Wood	Monkey
2005	9 February	Wood	Rooster
2006	29 January	Fire	Dog
2007	18 February	Fire	Pig
2008	7 February	Earth	Rat
2009	26 January	Earth	Ox
2010	14 February	Metal	Tiger
2011	3 February	Metal	Rabbit
2012	23 January	Water	Dragon
2013	10 February	Water	Snake
2014	31 January	Wood	Horse
2015	19 February	Wood	Sheep
2016	8 February	Fire	Monkey
2017	28 January	Fire	Rooster
2018	16 February	Earth	Dog
2019	5 February	Earth	Pig

The significance of the animals

Each animal has its specific attributes and, although Dragon is considered the luckiest, they are all essentially equal in worth. Every animal embodies a certain type of power or energy. This type of approach has its roots in shamanic culture. The shaman, or magical priest, would invoke the powers of animals as guides, guardians and allies in his journeys into the spirit world and each animal had a specific gift. A shaman might have one or two animals as his special Power Animals, drawing the spirit of the animal to him through ritual and also by dressing in the skin of the animal, or similar. Tribes would have animals as totems – a symbolic unifying principle that gave identity to the people.

THE RAT, SHU, SIGN OF CHARM

As Rat years mark the start of the 12-year cycle, they are considered auspicious for beginning any ventures. Regeneration and innovation are the order of the day. Improvements abound, the financial markets are buoyant and everything is on the up, including the spirits of the people. Plans should now be laid, projects commenced and new products launched. It is considered fortunate to marry in the year of the Rat. Starting a family, buying a house and generally re-inventing oneself and ones life are indicated, but instant results are by no means guaranteed and it is necessary to be very switched on, ready to adapt to changing conditions. The Rat is always active, always looking for the glittering prize. During this year there will always be opportunities for smart people to improve their lot, but recklessness is not advised, and Rat years bless the careful entrepreneur.

Rats can come up with original solutions in tight corners and have sharp intuition. For example, rats are very aware of impending danger and how to escape it. In days gone by there were few safeguards for people who worked in mines, and the miners depended on rats to warn them if there was a gas leak or an explosion threatening. If the rats were running, everyone knew it was time to get out. It was taboo to kill a rat and in some homes the rat had a similar status to the beloved Kitchen God, who protected the family (see Chapter 16).

There are few stories about rats in Chinese mythology, which is one reason why some scholars have asserted that the Zodiac is Indian in derivation. Another reason may be that the origins of the Zodiac are lost in the mists of time, along with stories that were part of an oral tradition, and which may have included the rat. One story tells how Cat and Rat were once sworn brothers, although they did have one or two disagreements. Both were invited to a party by the Jade Emperor (or the Buddha). Unfortunately, sleepy Cat forgot all about the event and did not attend. When Cat learned that Rat had been chosen to lead the 12-year cycle he became envious and spiteful, and ever since then he has chased Rat. This little story shows the dangers of arousing envy and that being singled out for favours may sometimes be a mixed blessing.

Individuals born in the year of the Rat like to take the lead. They are talented and need lots of stimulation. Wise and savvy, they can cope with a great deal, but their efficiency can sometimes tempt them into taking on too much. Curious, imaginative and insightful, Rats are a force to be reckoned with. They have charisma and a ready wit, and are approachable and genial. They do have some of the drawbacks associated with their animal: they can be secretive, greedy and devious.

The Rat 'hour' runs from 11 p.m. to 12.59 a.m., and this may be because that is the time of day when the creatures are most active. Rat is not really a rebel, but prefers to work cunningly within the system. Rats are active and highly-strung, but they nonetheless enjoy home and family. At work they have a sixth sense that enables them to be in the right place at the right time to make an impression and they are very ambitious. They seek new experiences and places, and love to talk about their travels – or indeed anything else. Rats will manipulate those they do not respect, but they are enduringly loyal to their true friends. The Rat month is December and Rat roughly corresponds to the Western sign of Sagittarius. This is the archetype of the Adventurer and the Seer, the person who thinks outside the box. The Rat represents the psychological drive to survive, to push the boundaries of experience, and to acquire assets as a bulwark against misfortune.

THE OX, NIU, SIGN OF INDUSTRY

After the élan of the Rat year, the following Ox 12 months are concerned with steady growth and stability. The new projects that were begun take root and there is time to gather the fruits of past efforts. However, this is no time to rest on one's laurels. Ox moves forwards, slowly but surely, and plans that have not been backed up with practical effort or contracts that have not been ratified may fall by the wayside. Traditional tastes, conservative values and a general reliance on the tried-and-tested work best in Ox years – the flashy and the daring may receive short shrift.

The Ox is a symbol for the success of the harvest, and is the focus for a Spring Equinox ritual, involving the agriculture god Mang Shen. Myth relates that Mang Shen beats a heavenly Ox with a willow branch every spring, in order to wake up the earth. This is symbolic of humans getting to grips with the land and making sacrifices to the powers of nature. A clay figure is made of Mang Shen and taken into the fields to be broken up and given to the soil. This may echo earlier rituals involving human sacrifice. Although the Ox is a beast, it is also a strong representation of the earth and fertility.

The 'beating' of the Ox may be interpreted as the intellect and conscious intent imposing its will on dumb nature, while the sacrifice aspect acknowledges that there is a price to pay (see also 'The Herdsman and the Weaver Girl', Chapter 14).

Individuals born in the Year of the Ox are reliable, hard-working and honest. They value integrity and sincerity, and are practical and realistic. They know there is no such thing as a free lunch and have scant patience with anyone who expects one. However, they will go out of their way to help their friends. Preferring the familiar, they are unlikely to set the world alight, yet they are determined and quietly ambitious. They may be stubborn and narrow-minded, yet they have hearts of gold and are very committed in relationships.

The Ox 'hour' runs from 1 a.m. to 2.59 a.m. These methodical people prefer to be prepared for all eventualities, and are generally early and focused on the task at hand. It is important to them to build a secure foundation, but although they are happiest working alone they need a caring family environment if they are to flourish. In partnerships they do like to be boss, and may be very deeply hurt by break-ups. They like to feel they are part of a dynasty, and are creatures of routine and hierarchy. The Ox month is January and the Western counterpart is Capricorn. This is the archetype of the Builder – the person who has the planning capability, and also the self-discipline, to make something step by step, out of basic materials. This may refer to a business or creative venture just as much as to bricks and mortar. The Ox is the psychological drive to master the environment and through this civilization moves onwards and upwards.

THE TIGER, HU, SIGN OF COURAGE

The Year of the Tiger comes in with a roar and demolishing anything that is not built on a very secure foundation. Things may happen out of the blue, giving individuals very little time to prepare or react rationally. Sometimes the effects of Tiger can be devastating, setting in motion a train of events that, rather like a house of cards falling, causes ongoing destruction. This is not a good time for the faint-hearted. People who are prepared to follow their intuition may do well now, and broad-brush schemes may succeed dramatically. However, failure is always a possibility and to make the best of Tiger years you need to thrive on the adrenaline rush. Feelings run high and there may be much emotional excitement, but anyone who plays with the hearts of others may find that their actions come back to bite them. On the positive side, this is a year for discovery, invention, resourcefulness and electrifying change, during which fortune favours the brave.

The Tiger is one of the Four Celestial Emblems associated with the four compass points. White Tiger resides in the West, and it was from this quarter that anything unpredictable or threatening was perceived to arrive. Attacking armies came from the West as did new and disturbing ideas. Dangerous, unpredictable, warlike and violent, Tiger energies need to be treated carefully in Feng Shui. While there does not appear to be a specific link between the White Tiger of the West and the Tiger of the zodiac, the beasts have characteristics in common. In Eastern Asia it is the Tiger, not the Lion, who is regarded as the King of the Beasts. The tiger bears a marking on its forehead that resembles the pictograph for 'king'. In Chinese folklore the were-tiger (as opposed to the werewolf) is an object of dread, not just because they might kill, but also because the soul of any individual eaten by a tiger would have to lure another victim to the tiger's lair before it could be released.

Those born in the Year of the Tiger are restless, passionate, impulsive and addicted to freedom. They cannot be controlled, and they like to dominate, yet they will respect anyone who confronts them, eye to eye. They thrive on challenge and they despise the petty and small-minded. Routine drives them crazy – they need to be on the prowl for interesting opportunities, ready to pounce when the time is right. In love they are passionate and, though commitment may come hard in youth, they make reliable and wholehearted partners in maturity.

The Tiger 'hour' runs from 3 a.m. to 4.59 a.m. Enthusiastic and optimistic, Tigers hate to miss anything and may quite angry if this happens – which luckily it seldom does! They can be arrogant and impatient, but they are nonetheless sociable and popular. Power and money do not impress them – they will take an individual on their own merits. Despite their enthusiasm they can feel temporarily destroyed by criticism or failure. The Tiger month is February and the Western counterpart is Aquarius. This is the archetype of the rebel, the person who challenges the accepted norm and is unafraid to tell it like it is, whatever the cost. The Tiger is a vital, if uncomfortable force – it prevents institutions from becoming calcified and sends human exploration and development off in fresh directions.

THE RABBIT, TU, SIGN OF PEACE

After the demands of the Tiger, a Rabbit year is like an oasis of calm. The healing influence of Rabbit can soothe away some of the traumas and dramas, bringing a chance to kick back and review the situation. There's no point getting all steamed up – trying to forge ahead in the Year of the Rabbit is rather like punching a cushion, with any dent you make soon disappearing. Instead, employ your energies subtly – negotiating, persuading and looking for points of agreement. Rabbit brings an essentially feminine outlook, focusing on home, family, security and health care. Medical matters are emphasized along with creativity and the arts generally.

The Rabbit may also be the Hare.

The Hare is often featured in Chinese cosmological art, mixing an immortality drug in a large bowl, so it has links with the Taoist quest for eternal life. This further emphasizes the magical quality of the creature, linking it to transformation and psychologically to the movement of unconscious elements within the mind into the light of consciousness. Hares can also signify sacrifice. One story tells of how the Lord Buddha met a hare while wandering alone and hungry in the forest. The hare told him to light a fire and prepare a pot. Even though he had nothing to cook, the Buddha followed the wishes of the creature. When the pan was bubbling the hare leapt into it, in order to feed the Master. Now unveiling his divine powers, the Buddha plucked the hare from out of the pot and set him in the moon, so that all might remember and honour his selflessness. ('Yi the Archer', Chapter 3, also links the hare with the moon.)

The Hare/Rabbit features prominently as the Jade or Gold Rabbit in an important Chinese festival – the Mid Autumn Moon Festival. It takes place on the fifteenth day of the Eighth Moon, which is the Full Moon closest to the Autumn Equinox. This is when for astronomical reasons, the moon appears at its largest – the so-called Harvest

Moon. This is a vibrant and magical occasion. Moonwatching parties are held, special mooncakes are eaten, lanterns are carried and incense is burned. The festival celebrates the harvest and, like so many events, honours the process of cycle within Nature.

Those born in the Year of the Rabbit are gentle and empathic. A quiet life and a peaceful one is their motto, and they do not meet trouble half way. Tactful well-mannered Rabbits are adept at getting on the right side of people. However, while they may appear altruistic, they are capable of carefully watching for a big opportunity. They also often go their own way and somehow manage to avoid upsetting anyone in the process. Pleasure-loving, artistic and playful, their sense of fun can sometimes be surprising. They can be deeply hurt by carelessness and criticism, although for their own sake and that of others they may hide this under a smile. Rabbits are stylish and well-groomed, and their resourcefulness means they often come up with a spot-on solution.

These crepuscular animals are happiest in the softer lights of dawn and dusk, so it is fitting that Rabbit 'hour' runs from 5 a.m. to 6.59 a.m. Rabbit is all urbane charm and finesse, appearing superficial when that suits the purpose. However, this is a personality of great depth that understands human foibles and misses very little of what is going on in the hearts and minds of companions. Sometimes they can be picky and possessive. Those born in Rabbit years adore their homes, handle money cleverly and advance in their careers through their excellent communication skills. Rabbit month is March and the Western counterpart is Pisces. This is the archetype of the saviour, who will put themselves last for the greater good (although the shadow side of this can be manipulative and guilt-tripping). Rabbit represents the cultural force that can transform and heal, sometimes when all seemed lost.

THE DRAGON, LUNG, SIGN OF LUCK

Dragon years are often dramatic and unforgettable. Magnificent Dragon announces the outlandish, the momentous and the highly original. The feel-good factor runs high and people are tempted to take risks. However, the Dragon is basically lucky, and experiences are exhilarating and often life-changing. Fortunes are made and lost in Dragon years, but even misfortune can be colourful. Fashion, culture and the arts receive a boost. Because this is considered the luckiest of the years, it is a favourite for marriages, new business initiatives, challenging projects and births. The Chinese expect significant international events to take place during the Year of the Dragon.

The Chinese Emperors regarded themselves as carriers of Dragon power, and sons of Heaven – the throne they sit on is the Dragon Seat, ceremonial robes are Dragon Robes and their beds are Dragon Beds. The Chinese sometimes describe themselves as 'the descendants of the Dragon'.

A story is told about a Chinese Lord Ye, who adored dragons. He thought about them constantly and surrounded himself with dragon motifs. One day a real dragon heard of his obsession and decided to pay him a visit. When Ye saw the mighty creature advancing on his dwelling he fell down dead with fright. This is a warning not to be sentimental and insincere and not to pretend to love that which you really fear.

Individuals born in Dragon years are often impressive. Sometimes they can be a little over-bearing, but there is something about them that commands respect. They love to be the centre of attention and are happiest when there is lots happening around them. These creatures were never made for routine. Independent and intuitive, they rely on themselves and while they are usually right, there are times when they would be better advised to take advice and look before they leap. They do not suffer fools gladly but are wonderful people to have in your corner – especially if it is a very tight one. They have enormous energy and will always go that extra mile to help a friend in need.

Dragon Hour runs from 7 a.m. to 8.59 a.m. when the daylight is new and strengthening, and efforts are getting underway. Dragons are endlessly enthusiastic and positive. Hugely generous, they are straight and trustworthy, but they are shrewd enough to avoid scams and freeloaders – Dragons help those who help themselves. Despite the fact that Dragons can be full of themselves, bossy and tactless, they usually inspire love and devotion because of their warmth and charisma. Slow to commit, they make devoted partners to someone who intrigues them and who can empathize. Dragon month is April and the Western counterpart is Aries. This is the archetype of the Pioneer, who fearlessly breaks new ground, having faith in himself and trusting to the Cosmos to favour him. He is the force in society that forges onwards and without which we would still be living in caves.

THE SNAKE, SHE, *SIGN OF WISDOM*

Snake years offer a quiet interlude to reflect on recent events – especially if these have been characterized by Dragon turbulence. Now it should be possible to re-establish routine and order, and to chill out. However, things are not always what they seem in Snake years. Much may be going on under the surface. Manipulation and misleading are possible as people keep their own counsel and further their own interests, so even straightforward matters need to be examined closely. The small print should be scrutinized and hidden agendas born in mind. In extreme cases, betrayal and conspiracy are fostered by the Snake vibe. There could be a few tabloid scandals, and issues linked with reproduction could make the news. However, the Chinese Snake does not carry the associations with evil and contemptibility that are common in the West. Instead, this reptile is a symbol of fertility and instinctual wisdom; if some underhand behaviour occurs this year, the message is wise up, so you don't become a victim. Snake years are considered favourable for finances, and fashion will reflect suave Snake style.

The symbolism of the snake was considered in the commentary to the myth of Wen Chang (Chapter 9).

Ancestors might appear in snake form, i.e. their root form, as the snake also represents the roots of the Tree of Life. Strongly intuitive and in touch with the wordless powers of the earth, Snake embodies influences that shape our lives but that we can often ignore. The Kundalini serpent is believed to reside at the base of the spine, and it relates to the energy of sexuality, which can be transformed into inner chi, or used to procreate.

Individuals born in the Year of the Snake are considered to be subtle and canny. They observe people and events apparently impassively, but they miss nothing and they sense exactly when to act. They know their own minds and usually get what they want with little effort. However, they can be hard to penetrate and while their air of mystery can be fascinating, people are sometimes made wary by their secretiveness and the fact they rarely trust. Although they love to party, they also enjoy their own company and need rest and seclusion. Passionate and highly-sexed, they can be disturbingly possessive at times.

Snake hour runs from 9 a.m. to 10.59 a.m. when the first rush at the start of the day has abated and activities are settled. Snakes are cool, yet deeply compassionate, and while they never forget a grudge their profound understanding of human nature gives them great empathy. They are mystical and psychic but also analytical, with a keen eye for detail and impressive organizational skills. The Western counterpart is Taurus, and while Snakes do display many Taurean characteristics, their magical quality is more reminiscent of Scorpio, Taurus' opposite in the Zodiac, which Taureans may express unconsciously. This is the archetype of the sower of seeds, the impulse to put down roots, both physically and in the realm of ideas. Culturally it represents stability and reflection, a turning inwards to assess one's place in the Universe, which often follows a dynamic phase.

Bai Suzhen

One story about a white snake is a Chinese favourite and has been turned into many operas and plays. It is set in the Southern Song Dynasty, 960–1279 CE. Bai Suzhen, a sinuous white snake from the Land of Demons, dreamed of becoming a goddess through doing kind deeds for others. She transformed herself into a woman and journeyed to the realm of the humans. She met a green snake called Qing who was causing havoc for the poor villagers who lived close to her lair. Outraged, and determined to fulfil her quest to save others, Bai imprisoned Qing at the bottom of a lake. However, kind-hearted Bai promised that she would return in 300 years, after Qing had learned her lesson, to free her. Bai continued on her travels, doing good wherever she went, and, true to her word, she returned to free Qing. The two snakes developed a sisterly affection for each other and all was going well until they met a magician called Fahai, who believed that all demons were evil and must be slain. Fahai challenged them but Bai was much too powerful, and Fahai resentfully retreated, promising himself that things would go differently next time they met.

However, Bai and Qing were now uneasy and for their own protection they decided to retreat to the Banbudno, a halfway realm between the demon and the human worlds. Both the snakes tried to continue their charitable work, but Qing made a mistake by flooding a parched area instead of bringing rains. Because of this, Bai assumed she had lost her chance of immortality, but the luminous goddess Kuan Yin appeared to her, comforted her and assured her she may have another opportunity.

The lives of the snake women became more complicated when, by accident, they magically transported a student named Xu Xian and his friend into the Demonland. Bai kept Xu safe, and fell in love with him, but she concealed her true identity fearing it would repel him. Xu had to battle the Lord of the Underworld in his travels, and after his ordeal he confessed that he had also loved Bai from the moment he first saw her. The lovers longed to be together in the human world, but no human can return to his own land from the Demon Realms without first having all his memory erased. Xu could not bear the thought of losing his link with Bai so he avoided becoming unconscious. But vengeful Fahai eventually caught up with them and he tricked Xu into being knocked out.

Returned to the human world, Xu forgot everything. He was separated from his friend, because they entered through a different portal, and Xu journeyed to find him, meeting many strangers in the process and becoming fully involved in his life once more. Meanwhile lonely Bai took her final step towards becoming a goddess by collecting the tears of humans. With her far-seeing eyes she spotted Xu with another woman and sorrowfully faced the fact she had lost him. But wise Qing knew that if Xu met Bai again he would fall in love with her once more. She arranged a meeting and the romance blossomed as planned. Xu and Bai were married, and they opened a medicine shop together.

Sadly, their happy-ever-after did not go as planned. Bonds between humans and demons are against natural law. The town fell victim to the plague and terrible destruction surrounded the loving couple. Bai, Qing and Fahai buried their differences and dedicated themselves to finding the magical help necessary for the suffering population. But Fahai was not to be trusted and even though Bai was pregnant with Xu's child he still plotted to destroy her and Qing.

According to Chinese custom, on the fifth day of the fifth lunar month any demons in human form must revert to their true shape. To escape from exposure, indefatigable Bai planned to take Qing and Xu back to Banbudno. But Fahai foiled their plans. Xu saw Bai in her true form and was literally scared to death. Bai found a magic potion that revived him but after the birth of their son she could bear the deception no more and she told him everything about her nature and origins. Faithful Xu declared that he would love her always, regardless, and the couple then hoped to resume a happy life together. But Fahai had been stalking them and, seeing that Bai was weak, attacked her, imprisoning her for all eternity beneath a pagoda.

COMMENTARY

This can be seen as a story of redemption of the animal and instinctual instincts, in the shape of the snakes, into a helpful and constructive force. The impulses we hide deep within us can be productive and creative if we can face them, transmute them and direct them consciously. Bai exemplifies the positive side of this while Qing retains her dark roots for longer. Fahai is the assertive analytical and logical element, eternally suspicious of the instinctual and at war with it. Xu is the loving force, the soul, that seeks unification and through him Bai can be redeemed – or can she? Bai can become a goddess –the powers of the primitive and the intuitive are to be revered and honoured, but when she tries to be human, the result is destruction. It is Qing, the more mischievous of the two, who brings about the doomed human–demon reunion. Qing is the alter ego of Bai, exemplifying the truly demonic, self-seeking and amoral side. Fahai, the ego, or conscious intellect, succeeds in vanquishing Bai and burying her for eternity. But has he truly won? Bai may be gone but she leaves a son, as proof of her potential, within the realm of humans.

THE HORSE, MA, SIGN OF ELEGANCE AND ZEAL

During Horse years things seem to happen at the gallop. There is a sense of lots going on, tempers flaring and subsiding, and the air crackling with expectancy. Commerce may flourish and anyone whose instincts are reliable will probably fall on their feet. A certain carelessness about the Horse means finances may be unstable and anyone who feels vulnerable should keep their purse closed. During Horse years debts may rise and economies fluctuate. Those who are easily bored will find they need the back door to be left open this year, or risk going stir-crazy. The outdoors is particularly attractive, with emphasis on leisure and travel. The madcap Horse encourages people to rush into tying the knot, but by the same token divorce is also likely, because anything past its sell-by date will be impatiently discarded.

The symbolism of the horse was looked at in the commentary on the story of the Silkworm Goddess (Chapter 10). The speed of the horse links it with those swift-as-lightning instincts which can help us reach goals much more quickly than by rational thought. By contrast, horses signify animal passion, which can waste time by charging headlong down blind alleys. Horses also symbolize the energy of the land, represented as ley lines. They are animals of passage, so not only does the Horse bring physical travel, it also relates to profound life changes. Some legends say that the Buddha had a horse called Kamthaka. This animal brings the spiritual message of karma. As karma is most properly understood as cause and effect, it is what propels us through life passages and incarnations.

Those born in the Year of the Horse are usually vivacious and popular. They have quick minds and are clever with words, but they do tend to speak the truth. Although they are ambitious they hate to be tied down and may suddenly rear up and gallop off if they feel too much is being demanded of them. They like to choose their own challenges and if something really appeals to them, they put huge amounts of energy into achieving success. Putting down roots does not interest them – they like to be able to canter off to pastures new and so their lives may be full of changes. In love they are impulsive and may enthusiastically repeat the same mistakes several times before they find The One.

Horse hour runs from 11 a.m. to 12.59 a.m., when the activities of the day are often at their most lively. Cheerful and witty, Horses are great companions, bringing a light-hearted atmosphere to any gathering. They can be refined and cultured but they do have a streak of selfishness and can sometimes be plain reckless. They quickly pick up new skills but may be prone to gamble with what they gain and with them it's 'easy come, easy go'. Their month is June and their Western counterpart is Gemini. This is the archetype of the mover and communicator. After projects have been thought up and put into practice, Horse embodies the drive to tell others, to recount stories and to move onwards to the next challenge. The Horse energy drives society outwards to fresh exploration.

The Good Luck Horse

An ancient Chinese story tells of the Good Luck Horse who brought the priceless gift of peace.

There was once a small boy called Wa Tung who longed to ride his father's horse. He so loved horses that he made one out of cloth and wished with all his heart it could be real. Little did he know that he was being watched by a cunning and powerful magician, who had a soft spot for childish imagination – which is, after all, the forerunner of magic. The magician changed the cloth horse into a real one. Wa Tung was ecstatic and rode his horse jubilantly around the garden. However, Wa Tung had forgotten to give his horse eyes. Totally blind, it trampled all the plants in his father's garden. His father was enraged and called the horse Bad Luck. Fortunately the magician spotted what had happened and he made the horse go backwards around the garden, undoing all the damage it had done. Wa Tung's father relented somewhat and renamed him Good-Luck-Bad-Luck, but the clumsy horse carried on breaking things, so the father banished him.

Good-Luck-Bad-Luck blundered off, but before long he met a mare called No-Good, and they got married. They lived happily but Good-Luck-Bad-Luck missed his master and so the two horses set off for Wa Tung's house. When they finally arrived they found Wa Tung preparing to go off to war against the enemy from the other side of the Wall. Good-Luck-Bad-Luck wanted to end this conflict once and for all. He consented to be Wa Tung's battle-horse, but Good-Luck-Bad-Luck managed to reason with the horses on the other side and convinced them to refuse to carry their masters into battle. 'Brothers, cousins, friends,' said the horse, 'we are all relations. I am married to one of you and all of you are wedded to my strength of purpose and my power. In war we suffer more than the humans, but today we shall not die. Instead we shall live. Let us carry our people, these foolish men, so close to one another that they will not be able to fight.'

And so peace was made and from that day Good-Luck-Bad-Luck was called simply 'Luck' and his wife was 'Luck's Wife'.

COMMENTARY

This happy story is a tribute to the simple ways of animals. It is also a vindication of the instincts, which often prompt us to depart from conditioning and the habits of our culture, and to see things with startling clarity. Sometimes if we have faith in this vision it can transform circumstances. The vivid, uninhibited imagination of childhood is what gives rise to this remarkable horse – play can be creative and provide a powerful vehicle for moving onwards. In some myths horses can be sinister creatures, carrying underworld deities or taking the hapless rider along the road to hell. The magical horse was first destructive because it was blind – which is exactly how instincts can be. However, this story shows that the horse energy, when used wisely, can bring good fortune.

THE SHEEP, YANG, SIGN OF THE ARTS

The pace moderates as Sheep ambles in, and peace and calm reign. Home, family, falling in love, marrying and having babies are all now favoured. In the world at large tranquillity is more likely as bridges are built between dissenting factions. Diplomacy, tact and reconciliation spread their soothing influence over all. This is not a great time for new ventures – better to work on what is established and make it more secure and profitable. Humanitarian and green concerns receive extra attention as awareness grows of the importance of the welfare of humans, animals and the planet. Charitable organizations are supported and medical matters advance. Gentle Sheep makes everyone feel reassured, stable and relaxed.

The Chinese word *Yang* also translates as Ram or Goat. There is a story of how the Five Rams of Canton brought nourishment to the world. According to tradition, over 2,000 years ago five immortals dressed in robes of the five colours (black, white, yellow, green and red) descended from heaven, each seated on a ram of the same colour as their robes. Each of the rams carried a grain of rice in its mouth. They came to earth in Canton, and where they touched the ground they each turned into a standing stone. However, the grains of rice remained unchanged. From these the people learned the secrets of farming, and the five grains flourished into abundant crops. This story probably relates to a stone circle that is even more ancient than the legend. This circle has vanished and a monastery was built on the spot, which has in turn been demolished. A Taoist temple of the Five Immortals still stands in the vicinity.

This story could be interpreted as portraying the idea that fertility (possibly of mind and body/earth) comes from a union of land and sky. The five immortals wear specific colours, which indicate they carry a specific energy. Red and green are the colours of life, as in foliage and blood respectively. To the Chinese yellow is a colour associated with death, while black and white are night and day. So the process of cyclic life is depicted and honoured. This is in keeping with the year of the Sheep.

People born in the year of the Sheep have two speeds – slow and stop. If they are pushed they may dig in their heels in or become upset. They like security but they can be flexible, adjusting to the needs and demands of others as long as these are not too onerous. Charming and obliging, they love to be surrounded by supportive companions, but they do not wear their hearts on their sleeve. This is for self-protection, but it can be counter-productive because others do not always know what motivates Sheep and may unintentionally hurt or hinder them. If this happens Sheep can become very wounded and moody. They have endless sympathy for anyone who is down – their own shy and timid streak gives them understanding of the vulnerable. Sheep find their greatest happiness in a loving partnership, with a comfortable home and family providing a cushion against life's knocks.

The Sheep month is July and the Sheep 'hour' is 1 p.m. to 2.59 p.m. – this is the time when many people have lunch and there may be a little postprandial sleepiness. Sheep people are strongly artistic – they have no wish for power or prominence, yet they sometimes have greatness thrust upon them because of their talents. At their worst they can be sulky, fussy and self-indulgent but their sweet natures usually ensure that they are quickly forgiven. Although rarely flamboyant, they are outrageous spendthrifts and generally look well-heeled. At work they are happiest in a supportive role and Sheep really come into their own when they have their 'other half' to encourage them to shine. The Western counterpart of Sheep is the sign of Cancer. This represents the cultural impulse to create a home and family, and to build a safe haven in which to develop.

THE MONKEY, HOU, *SIGN OF IMAGINATION*

Hitches and hiccups, detours and distractions – few things go as planned in the Year of the Monkey. Sometimes they may turn out better than expected, sometimes worse, but there is often an impression of Fate playing games. The unforeseen inevitably happens and even though we may try hard to cover every eventuality there is always one thing that is overlooked and comes back to bite us. It is important to have back-up strategies and insurance in place for everything in the Year of the Monkey. Markets are unstable and international affairs variable. Monkey years favour those who can think on their feet and don't mind changing plans at the drop of a hat. There is a forward-looking, bubbly feel during this year that favours anything requiring quick wits and nimble fingers.

Monkey is a key figure in Chinese myth and his lengthy story is covered in Chapter 11.

The festival to Sun Wukong the Monkey King is celebrated on the sixteenth day of the eighth lunar month of the Chinese calendar, which falls in September/October. Events feature some of his ordeals such as fire-walking and climbing a ladder of knives. Incense and paper offerings are burned as a tribute. Monkey King's saga is a story of redemption and the journey of the Hero.

People born in the Year of the Monkey are bright and mischievous. They see no harm in being creative with the truth when it suits them and they can usually talk their way out of the tight corners they land in. It is hard to catch them out – they assess situations and adapt to them with lightning speed, turning everything to their advantage. Nosy and irrepressible, Monkeys gather a following of fascinated hangers-on but there are also those who never trust them. This is a little unfair, for Monkeys are not malevolent. They are interested in a wide variety of subjects and often switch course on impulse, in a way that can be bewildering to slower souls. Often they are good at languages. A steady routine is death to them – they need a stimulating environment that will present them with varying challenges.

The Monkey month is July and the Monkey 'hour' is 3 p.m. to 4.49 p.m., which is good for assessing the various elements that have arisen during the day and finding resourceful solutions. Monkeys are imaginative and ingenious. They have a blinding sense of humour and the ability to sell snow to Eskimos. They are not the most faithful of partners and when young they flirt continuously. Having sown their wild oats, however, Monkeys will dedicate their fantastic ingenuity to keeping a committed relationship spicy. The Western equivalent is Leo and Monkey emphasizes the playful and creative aspect of that sign. In society Monkey represents that invaluable force that prevents stagnation and that keeps alive the questioning attitude of the child. Complacency stultifies progress – Monkey is dedicated to ensuring that never happens.

THE ROOSTER, JI, SIGN OF HONESTY

Rooster years look onwards and upwards with confidence. Those who have a proper sense of self-worth prosper this year. It is an especially good time for the repressed and abused to cast off their shackles and demand their rights – bullies beware when the Rooster comes to town! Criticism will be rife, however, and anyone who is having trouble in a relationship will find it hard to paper over the cracks now. Image-conscious Rooster is favourable for makeovers and keeping up with the Joneses. There is a touch of the flamboyant and also the wish to feather one's nest with pride and dignity.

Those born in the Year of the Rooster are often proud and attention-seeking, although they are not characteristically foolish and careless like the rooster in the story that follows – in fact they like to make detailed plans and to be prepared for all eventualities. They work hard and are very efficient, although they tend to sweat the small stuff and tangle themselves in red tape. Roosters tell it like it is and while this may not always be comfortable, at least you know exactly where you stand. They do not suffer fools gladly or ill-treatment. In their element on social occasions, Roosters invest a lot of time and energy in looking their best. They love to dress up in their finest feathers and make an impression.

The Rooster's month is September and its 'hour' is 5 p.m. to 6.59 p.m., when birds are returning to their nests. This is in contrast to the western image of the rooster, greeting the dawn. The Western counterpart to the sign is Virgo, and while the ostentation of the Rooster may not seem to fit, Virgo does have a great pride in doing things well and looking its best. Roosters are practical and logical, willing to graft and climb the ladder of promotion. Bossy and uncompromising, they keep their most tender feelings under wraps and never kiss-and-tell. Rooster represents the cultural need to organize and administrate, keeping the complications of civilization manageable and setting a firm basis for future growth.

The Dragon and the Rooster's crown
In this version of the story about how the Dragon got the Rooster's crown, the Buddha, or Jade Emperor, informed the animals that

he would be choosing 12 of them each to give their name to a year. The Dragon was worried – he knew he was magnificent but he was concerned that his dull, brown head would cause him to lose out.

'If only I had a wonderful head-dress the Buddha would be sure to choose me' he hissed to himself. He went to his friend Centipede to make a deal with him. 'If you can get me Rooster's fabulous head-dress' he said, 'I will make you powerful and swift like me.'

How could Centipede refuse? He crawled up to Rooster, being careful to hide behind rocks and stones in case Rooster got mad and decided to peck him to death. But Rooster was in a good mood.

'Ha! So old Fire-breath wants my crown, does he?' crowed Rooster. 'Well, I can be generous. Here you are Centipede, Dragon can borrow it.' He placed his shimmering head-dress on Centipede's back. 'Make sure you return it to me, you hear.' And Rooster strutted cockily away.

Centipede went back triumphantly to Dragon, who promptly did just as he had promised. He made Centipede strong and dangerous with powerful legs and a poisonous sting. But he also gave Centipede some good advice about being modest and cautious.

In the following few days the years were named and sure enough, Dragon was among them. So was Rooster but he wasn't at all happy. 'I should have been chosen before Dragon' he complained very loudly. 'Give me back my crown!'

'It suits me much better,' replied Dragon, 'and anyway, Centipede said I could keep it.' Rooster was furious and stalked off to find Centipede.

'You tricked me!' he squawked. Centipede wasn't afraid. He was now powerful, and could fight and sting. But he remembered what Dragon had told him – after all, Rooster had a very sharp beak. So he decided it would be more prudent to avoid trouble, and slipped under a stone. Rooster knew he was beaten so he flew off to the heavens to join the others and make the best of a bad job. But ever since then Rooster has wished for his beautiful, shining crown and it is around Dragon hour that you will hear a rooster crowing his lament for his lost treasure.

COMMENTARY
This legend illustrates that pride goes before a fall. It is Rooster's over-confidence that costs him his crown. The magical (if duplicitous)

Dragon gives the message 'Be modest' when he grants power to the Centipede. Rooster's arrogance makes him careless. If one has something special it is wise not to flaunt it in front of powerful creatures (e.g. dragons). In other words, don't tempt Fate. In psychological terms, an inflated ego may tend to claim gifts of Nature as its own achievement, rather than appreciating them with gratitude and using them as a blessing to all – these gifts may include intelligence, wealth or beauty. When that happens there is always the risk that the gift will be in some way spoilt or rendered useless just when the individual most needs it.

THE DOG, GOU, *SIGN OF FAITHFULNESS*

Caring for others and standing by your community, family and ideals are the priority in Dog years. Environmental issues are likely to be debated and addressed, along with human rights. Compassion and benevolence bring a welcome relief from cut-and-thrust – companies and institutions are more likely to take on board the fact that people really work better and produce more when they are happy and well-treated. 'Is this fair?' is a prime question in Dog year. Animal welfare is also of major concern. Internationally and domestically the emphasis is on defence and security. If you have something that needs to be or should be protected, Dog year will guide you. This is a good year to ask yourself what you truly value in life and what brings you fulfilment, and to make more time and space for it. Background anxiety should not become neurosis – be clear about priorities and maintain equilibrium.

Dog has always been 'man's best friend'. Dog is also a guardian of the threshold and is a pseudonym for guidance, protection and loyalty. Like all animals he represents instincts which help to connect us with nature, and with his ability to round up domestic livestock and hunt wild beasts he is a significant symbol of a healthy relationship between the primitive and the civilized. Dog's excellent nose is linked to intuition, which 'sniffs out' when something isn't quite right. But Dog can also mean aggression and such figures as the Hounds of Hell may denote dark forces in the unconscious mind. These need to be faced if a person is to progress in wisdom, so Dog stands guard at the boundaries of consciousness and like so many beasts has links with the process of initiation.

The Fu Dog is a familiar Chinese figure. This dog resembles a lion and is often black. It has immense protective powers, standing guard at the entrances to palaces, temples, tombs and offices. Fu Dog was a favourite companion of the Buddha. These dogs appear in pairs, one on either side of the door, representing male and female and the balance that is Dog's characteristic. Fu Dog brings happiness and good fortune, and banishes evil spirits. However, the Chinese concept of dogs is not all positive and it is believed to be the Celestial Dog that eats the sun at eclipses.

The black dog as a symbol for depression is well known. Depression often takes place when repressed emotions or contents from the unconscious are striving to make themselves known. So the spark of life and ego that is symbolized by the Sun is eaten by this threshold guardian, who is in effect an emissary of the primitive instincts. This may seem negative and scary, which indeed it can be, but dog energies in this case may simply be trying to allow darkness, i.e. the unconscious, to express itself so the personality can be more rounded, balanced and potent. The Dog is especially honoured on Day 2 of the Chinese New Year, as a friend and support to humans. This day is considered to be the birthday of all dogs.

Individuals born in the Year of the Dog are loyal and reliable. Their cheerful air and frank but pleasant manners make them very popular. They have a very strong sense of justice and they stubbornly decline to do anything that they consider immoral or unfair. Helping others is their primary concern, but if they are hurt they lick their wounds for a long time and they are capable of holding quite a strong grudge until they receive an apology or compensation – even then they may not forget in a hurry. Switched on and watchful, Dogs are quick to see which way the wind blows and good at taking appropriate action. They identify the problems and dig up a good solution, but they can be worriers and hard to reassure when they sense trouble. Calm in a crisis, Dogs can still occasionally lose their temper for something apparently trivial but as long as they aren't baited they soon move on. Sometimes Dogs can be pessimistic, negative and cynical. These people are good at small talk and attached to their circle of friends. They are especially contented when they have a settled partnership, and they are faithful for life.

Dog 'hour' is 7 p.m. to 8.59 p.m. – a time special to families, when everyone may be gathered around the hearth or sharing the evening meal. Dog month is October and the Western counterpart is Libra, sign of the Scales. Dog's insistence on fairness is classic Libra, along with concern for others and a preoccupation with high standards. This is the archetype of the judge and arbiter. Culturally it is the impulse that assesses what is for the greater good, and that weighs things up so that what is best may receive attention and enable further progress to take place.

THE PIG, ZHU, SIGN OF HONESTY

Pig is the final year of the cycle, so this is a time for winding things up and putting everything in order. Although there is a sense of things coming to an end, Pig brings a positive outlook. There is an expectation of abundance, good times and smooth achievement. Laid-back Pig encourages self-indulgence. Leisure industries thrive, restaurants flourish and people manage to splash out on more luxury goods. This year isn't about lazing around and neglecting fitness, however. Pig brings respect for the body, and sports often do well now. It may be easier than usual to enjoy yourself in the Year of the Pig and as long as you don't take the Pig's tendency to gamble to extremes, finances should be on the up and stress on the down.

In the West the Pig is often regarded as a dirty, greedy animal. However, pigs, when well-treated, are extremely clean and wholesome. This animal is a symbol of nourishment, generosity and abundance. The hedonistic character of the Pig leads to happy discoveries about life, and thus to creativity and inspiration. This 'mental fertility' is paralleled by the pig's physical fertility, but the Pig can also symbolize the animal instinct to run amok. The term 'pig-headedness' refers to stubbornness, and Pig may represent elements in the unconscious mind that stand in the way of transformation and moving on. These may include desires and habits we cling to, instinctively, although we know they are unproductive. The sow breeds a litter but if conditions are not favourable she may eat the piglets. Because of this Pig may be associated with the passage of time, which brings things into being, transforms and then destroys, making Pig a fitting animal to end the sequence.

People born under the sign of the Pig are souls of generosity, good humour and kindness. Their sense of fun is irrepressible, but their jokes are rarely at the expense of others. Pigs enjoy a good time and if possible they will live out their lives in the lap of luxury. They love their homes and will often spend time and money making these comfortable, welcoming and beautiful – although they are not always the best at housework. These people are good organizers, hard workers, reliable, patient and with loads of stamina. Sometimes they are materialistic, stubborn and lazy. They can occasionally be gullible because they assume others are as trustworthy as they are. Pigs are sensualists – they adore good food and good sex. Life's simple pleasures make them happy.

Pig 'hour' is from 9 p.m. and 10.59 p.m., when everyone is settling down, indulging in snacks and preparing for bed. The Western counterpart is Scorpio, and Pig month is November. Pig's sensuousness is recognizably Scorpionic but many of Pig's other characteristics are more reminiscent of Taurus, the sign in polarity to Scorpio (it is interesting to note that Snake, the Chinese counterpart to Taurus, is more like Scorpio). Although Pig's concern with the material might be termed superficial, by tasting all of life's sweetness Pig may exemplify a pagan spirituality which views the material as a route to the Divine, rather than something to be risen above. Pig's sensuousness is an act of worship of the powers of life. This is the cultural element that rewards and enjoys. When the work is done, the fruits of the labours are there to be relished. There may be a profound wisdom to living in the moment and Pig brings the cycle to a close in mindfulness and repose.

The pigs and the stars
A story linking pigs with kindness concerns the wise astrologer I-hsing, who lived from 672–717 CE, and was prophet to the Emperor Hsuan Tsung. When I-hsing was studying he was very poor, and he owed some of his success to the care of a widow called Wang-mu. Later, when I-hsing had received his court appointment, the widow came to him weeping piteously. Her son had been convicted of manslaughter and was to be executed. I-hsing assured her that her son would be saved. He went to a nearby temple where he rented a room, in which he placed a large jar. Then he informed the temple attendant that on a certain day at a certain time seven animals would stray into the temple precinct. The attendant was to make sure he caught them in a bag. The man, sworn to secrecy, promised to comply, and at the selected time he watched the temple garden. Sure enough, seven little pigs ran in among the flowers and were duly caught. The servant called I-hsing who rewarded him, transferring the piglets to the glass jar, which he then sealed with certain mysterious symbols. The next day, much to the consternation

of the palace and the populace, the imperial astronomer announced that the seven major stars of the Great Bear had disappeared. This was a very bad omen, so the Emperor summoned I-hsing to ask his advice. The prophet told the Emperor that the only way to bring back the stars would be to grant general amnesty to all prisoners. Without hesitation the Emperor agreed. Each day one of the piglets was released and one of the stars reappeared in the Great Bear. The widow's son was set free and everyone was happy.

COMMENTARY
This story shows how forgiveness and empathy restore the natural order, as represented by the pigs. Such impulses within humans are one of the elements that hold society together and make our shared lives fulfilling.

16

The Kitchen God and Chinese New Year

Tsao Chun, or Tsao Wang, also called the Kitchen God or the Stove God, is one of the most popular and universally worshipped of all Chinese deities, and was once represented in every household. There are many stories about him. One relates how a man named Chang Tsao-wang married a virtuous and gentle maiden called Kuo Ting-hsiang. She was faithful and hard-working and did her best to make him happy, keeping the house clean and tidy, and cooking the most delicious meals. During their relationship the fortunes of Chang flourished, but he was not contented. He fell in love with another woman, Li Hai-T'ang – a selfish femme fatale who persuaded him to divorce his wife and marry her instead. However, separated from Ting-hsiang, Chang did not do well. Bad luck dogged him and his finances dwindled. This was a great disappointment to Li Hai-T'ang, who abandoned him. Chang was ruined, and his health suffered. He lost his sight and took to begging from door to door. One day he smelt a particularly delicious aroma of cooking. Following his nose he knocked hopefully on the door, and was welcomed into the warm interior where he was fed a dish of noodles. Chang began to weep, saying they were as satisfying as those his former wife used to make. He had actually strayed into the dwelling of Ting-hsiang, who then joyfully recognized him.

'Chang Lang, Chang Lang,' she cried 'open your eyes!' Immediately Chang recovered his sight, and realized where he was. Instead of being jubilant he was overcome with guilt, and threw himself into the roaring hearth, where he was burned to death. Ting-hsiang tried to save him by grasping his leg but it came away from his burning body.

Ever since then the rake used for ashes in China has been called Chang Lang's leg.

Commentary

This is a cautionary tale about the evils of disloyalty. However, the tale of the Kitchen God is one of the most important in Chinese culture, allied as it is with the New Year celebrations.

The Kitchen God is represented by a paper image pinned over the stove and renewed each year, or he may be present as a small clay figure kept in a niche by the stove. Some households have an entire shrine to him and he is a culturally beloved figure.

SACRIFICIAL GOD

This story may also echo traditions of a sacrificial god who is cut down in order that the life of the earth shall continue.

These deities are often slain by the hand of the goddess herself, for she embodies the inexorable cycle, while the male deity represents life that surges and retreats. In such tales the goddess sorrows for her fallen lover even though she acknowledges the necessity for his demise. In the story of the Kitchen God, two women, i.e. two aspects of the Feminine, are instrumental in his death, hinting at the importance of feminine (instinctual) power.

THE THEME OF EATING

Necessary for survival and often central to celebrations, eating is one of life's pleasures. However, eating also has the symbolic meaning of taking in the outside world and 'digesting' experience. It is when Chang eats the noodles that he becomes aware of what he has done with his life. At this point he really comes down to earth and faces the consequences of his actions.

BETRAYAL

Chang betrays his wife and is then in turn betrayed by his mistress. Betrayal is an inevitable fact of life but in stories such as this it hints at the darker side of the personality and at unconscious elements which have not been able to be made conscious, and so transform into something effectual. At first Chang struggles to bring his life and his ideals together, and what happens within him is a betrayal of the self, as he is not able to grow into a responsible, mature and fulfilled partner. Light – quite literally – dawns on Chang when he realizes that his first wife is there (representing a higher part of his personality) and that there might be a possibility of redemption. Although the story now recounts that he threw himself into the fire out of remorse, fire itself is a transformative element.

Chinese New Year

The Chinese New Year is a luni-solar festival, defined by the cycles of Sun and Moon. It falls on the second new moon after the Winter Solstice. Many cultures have striven to combine the cycles of sun and moon in their calendar. This may be seen as an attempt to harmonize Yin and Yang, masculine and feminine, as represented by the sun and the moon. The English word 'month' derives from 'moon' but the western calendar only pays lip-service to the lunar cycles, whereas the Chinese time the start of each year by them. This means that Chinese New Year starts on a different date each year, in a 19-year cycle.

Chinese New Year is a very important festival, celebrated throughout East and South-east Asia, and also where ethnic Chinese are grouped. It is a brilliant and atmospheric occasion, central to the mythic life of the Chinese. The Kitchen God makes his departure during the week before New Year and his paper effigy is burned outside by the head of the family. Despite the fact that the kitchen is the province of the female head of the household, the worship of the Kitchen God is the preserve of the male head of the household, sometimes even excluding female family members. This may possibly be seen as a vestige of masculine initiation rites.

So that the Kitchen God may pay a visit to the Gods of the Western paradise and tell them what the family have been doing, his paper image is taken down and ceremoniously burned. Sometimes a little straw is included for his horse, some honey to give him a sweet taste and some alcohol so he can be pleasantly tipsy and more inclined to give a good report of the household. The alcohol also has the advantage of making the fire burn a bit brighter. Sometimes a priest is called in, for extra good fortune. If the house has an altar to the Kitchen God, this is transported outside and a table laid with cakes and goodies. Incense is smouldered and fireworks set off prior to the burning of the effigy.

There are a host of other New Year customs. People seek to have their fortune told, and flock to the temples to pray for things to go well in the coming year and seek advice. Before New Year, homes are cleared out and 'floor sweeping day' is held. After the Kitchen God has been sent on his way, presents are given and flower fairs begin. All business transactions have to be sorted and debts discharged. Food has to be prepared in advance because it is unlucky to use scissors or knives on New Year's Day. Foods are chosen for their symbolic associations or for the sound of their names: for instance carp may be served because it symbolizes long life; lettuce and cabbages may appear on the menu because their names sound like the words for 'fortune' and 'riches'.

Children stay up late to see the New Year in, and poems, written on strips of red paper, are stuck over door lintels. Before midnight the doors are sealed, to be opened at dawn when incense is offered to the powers of land and sky. Family get-togethers follow. Gifts of money are given in red packages and fireworks are set off, to frighten evil spirits. A green branch may be burned to affirm the passing of the old year. A time of inactivity follows, because it is unlucky to clean or sweep for two days, lest all the good fortune be swept away. It is important not to fall down or to break anything, as that would be an evil omen.

The second day is devoted to visiting, with lots of gambling and entertainment. On the third day it is customary to consult an oracle, called *chim*. This is a popular way of getting in touch with one's ancestors. Many families have their own chim – a cylindrical container filled with numbered bamboo strips, often with an accompanying book of interpretations. On the following day the beloved Kitchen God is welcomed back and a new picture of him is attached to the hearth. New Year's Day is everyone's birthday and Chinese people used to count their age from the New Year in which they were born, rather than from the day they were born. This may be partly due to the fact that the Chinese sense of being part of a community is strong, and the need to be a separate individual is not so intense. The Chinese New Year is a time for reconciliation and a sincere wish to forget all grudges and to be warm and close.

Conclusion

Chinese thought differs from the Western outlook in many respects. In particular, the Chinese apparently possess a greater sense of the community, and are less devoted to individualism. To explore this difference has not been part of the purpose of this book, which has attempted, rather, to draw from the myths what may be applicable to us today in the West. This is not only justified by analytical psychological approaches, which state that myth is a product of the collective unconscious. It is also supported by the attitude of the Chinese themselves to their mythology, which is tolerant and eclectic, embracing many beliefs. Thus a temple in Hong Kong, for instance, might be dedicated to a specifically Buddhist or Taoist figure, but it is far more likely to enshrine many diverse figures, and as such to be supported by the local community. Teaching centres or monasteries are often much more specialized, but these are less commonly encountered.

There is no term in Chinese for an omnipotent, single deity, and this was a difficulty encountered by the first Christian missionaries. However, there exists a notion of a cosmic order, and a belief that when Earth is in harmony with Heaven, peace prevails, and when this is not the case, disasters strike. Thus there is a sense of the homogenous nature of the universe which partakes of the notion of the Tao and could be looked upon as the existence of a supreme power. Taoism, in its more accessible form, regards this 'power' as administered by an extensive hierarchy of heavenly bureaucrats, giving every small thing and idea its own special deity. However, in contrast with Western concepts, the earliest Chinese ideas which lie at the root of Taoism regard the universe and its creation in an abstract fashion. At the beginning of time was the Great Monad; from the Monad emerged duality, and from thence the Ten Thousand Things.

Even within the vast throng of deities and spirits there remains an abstract core. The God of Astrology, for instance, found in many temples along with his 60 attendants, has a home that is purely hypothetical. He is believed to inhabit the point in space where the planet Jupiter would be if it travelled in the direction opposite to that which it actually follows! Every thought and action that can be named has its own spirit. This makes for a colourful and adaptable approach. It also can be regarded as an awareness of the world of spirit that interpenetrates the physical, portrayed in a literal and vivid fashion.

As we have seen, Chinese myth is of its nature complex and multi-faceted. To this is added the vastness and cultural variety within the Chinese subcontinent, the various influences from India and other foreign cultures, the fact that historical personages have been mixed with deities, and that all tales have been written and rewritten in a continuous and interweaving process. In addition, there is comparatively little material available in translation. All these factors mean that what we see of Chinese myth is only a glimpse. Myths, however, were never intended to be strictly classified, identified and dissected – not, that is, if we wish to get the most out of them. They are ideas to play with, to expand our awareness and to bring to life that which is difficult to comprehend in a logical fashion.

The Chinese themselves have adapted their myths, grafting the old onto the new in a continuous process of creation. Our use of them in this book has aimed to be one of creative application, in a spirit of respect for the richness and wisdom of the Chinese culture.

Appendix 1: Feng Shui

There are several ancient works that describe the basic tenets of Feng Shui. One is the *Shih Ching*, or *Book of Songs*, which was compiled over a period between c.800 BCE and 400 BCE. Another is known as the *Li Chi*, or *Book of Rites*, written during the Han dynasty, between 206 BCE and 220 AD. These works are based on Taoism, the ancient and well-developed spiritual philosophy of China (see Introduction).

Everything that can possibly be known arises from the Tao. According to the Taoists, the Universe can be divided into Heaven and Creation, which can also be called spirit and matter. These are represented respectively as a circle and a square. The circle is regarded as Yang, and its representation was resolved into an unbroken line – this represents Heaven. The square is matter, physical Creation, which is Yin, and this was developed into a broken line.

Combinations of Yin and Yang, represented by broken/unbroken lines, also form the divination system, the I Ching (see Appendix 2).

Feng Shui is a cultural narrative rather than a story, bringing a vibrant, mythical life to the environment. While individual myths may be interpreted in terms of the subconscious mind, and its secret dramas, Feng Shui is the ongoing subtle energy fluctuations in a world where reality is not quite what it may seem.

The Five Elements are employed in Feng Shui, both to suit the house to the personality and to draw in certain qualities: for instance, the ideal house faces south, because that draws in light and warmth, while the master bedroom is best placed in the west, encouraging relaxation.

The Ba Gua and Lo Shu

In Feng Shui the space to be considered is divided up into nine areas. These correspond to the eight directions of the compass, along with a central point, symbolizing balance, stability and harmony with the earth. The octagonal diagram called the Ba Gua depicts this, showing eight equal segments with the ninth space at the centre sometimes displaying the Yin/Yang sign. On the Ba Gua the eight directions each show one of the trigrams of the I Ching (see Figure 4.1). The Ba Gua itself lies at the heart of Feng Shui, for it can be used as a 'map' placed over the plan of an area or building, so that the different parts of the structure can be related to different energies/areas of life. For instance the south-east corner is related to money and riches (although most Feng Shui practitioners these days orient the Ba Gua relative to the front door, equating that with North, which means, for instance, that the money corner is always at the far left of the entrance).

The Ba Gua translates into/arises from the Lo Shu, or 'magic square', showing nine segments. 'Lo Shu' means 'Book of the River'. Each segment is numbered in such a way that in whatever direction you add the numbers, whether up, down or diagonally, you arrive at the number 15. This can be seen as representing an underlying harmony and cosmic patterning, accessed in Feng Shui.

The Lo Shu is some of the oldest magic known. It appears in the Western tradition as the Saturn square – so called because Saturn is related to the third sephirah on the Qabalistic Tree of Life, and this magic square contains three rows of three figures. Saturn is a planet/force connected with boundaries and solidity. The Tree of Life is a 'diagram of manifestation' connecting purest spirit with densest matter. The Qabalah is completely separate from Chinese mythology, but the link is interesting.

Putting Feng Shui into practice

The things we surround ourselves with are not merely 'things' – they have an essence, a symbolic quality, and they affect the flow of unseen energy, called *chi*. Chi needs to move freely, but not in too hectic a fashion. Rooms need to be balanced with consideration for the 'vibrations' in specific areas. The concept of Yin and Yang underlies Feng Shui, but when applied properly it is a complex system. 'Feng Shui' means 'Wind, Water' and Feng Shui principles arise from the unseen powers of Nature.

True Feng Shui is a matter of deep study and long practice, but there are some basic observations and small actions that can sometimes have pleasing effects.

As we have seen, each of the nine segments in the Ba Gua, or Lo Shu, relates to an area of life, providing a plan to assess the characteristics of the space and how it will affect the occupants. Specifically, Segment One relates to success and career, appearing in the north. To its right, in the north-east, is Segment Eight, relating to knowledge and effectuality. Going round the Ba Gua in a clockwise direction we come to the east: Segment Three connects with family; Segment Four appears in the south-east, and means wealth. Directly south lies Segment Nine, signifying fame and reputation, South-west houses Segment Two, relationships and marriage; Segment Seven lies in the west and relates to offspring, and coming to the north-west and Segment Six we arrive in the area of friends and helpful people. In the centre is Segment Five, the Tai Chi, or Supreme Potential. However, please note that the meanings of the segments do vary somewhat, according to different sources.

If you place the Ba Gua over a diagram of your house you will be able to see what goes where. For instance you will be able to locate your marriage segment and if things aren't going well in your relationships you might like to examine that area. Is it cluttered and messy? Or maybe it looks sparse and empty. You can immediately alter the Feng Shui by rearranging the relevant segment. According to Chinese tradition, change will soon follow in your life. A mini-version of this can also be applied to a room, or even a desk.

Once you have the general idea of Feng Shui you can begin to experiment. It is very important not to make major changes or to expect swift results – it may take several weeks or months for a shift to take place. It is also important to remember the rule 'if it's not broken, don't fix it'. It may be tempting to rearrange every area of your life and in so doing cause upheaval – Feng Shui should be carefully targeted.

Feng Shui can be used to help balance a personality. For instance, if practicalities trip you up, tidy up your far left corner, i.e. Segment Four, your wealth area. Place a few coins there and/or a money plant. If your relationships don't thrive, clear up your Segment Two in the far right, and place pairs of objects there, such as two doves, two teddy bears or whatever appeals. If you don't seem to have much drive, make sure your entrance is clear in Segment One and that as you come in your front door you have a feeling of smooth movement, successful entry. If you want children or yearn to explore life's mysteries and create transformation, place an ear of wheat in Segment Seven, in the right of your dwelling. Family and joy can be boosted by a lamp in Segment Three on the left, knowledge and power may be enhanced by books and trophies in the near left hand Segment Eight, while Segment Nine, straight ahead could be a good place for a symbol of success, such as the sun. Place presents from friends in Segment Six, on your right as you come in. Segment Five, in the centre, might be a good place for your computer.

Stand at your doorway and imagine you are the life force, or *chi* – where would you flow freely? Where might you get stuck, or rush too fast? You can adjust this with lamps, wind-chimes, plants, ornaments and crystals. Of course most homes are not square, and there may even be segments that seem missing – for instance if your dwelling is an 'L'-shape. Invoke the energies of the missing section by placing appropriate artefacts close to where it should be.

The importance of Feng Shui

The Ba Gua also has associations with the calendar months, animals, times of the day and more. Awareness of Feng Shui is central to Chinese culture, most buildings and even the city of Beijing was built according to these principles.

Appendix 2: The I Ching and the Eight Trigrams

The I Ching

The I Ching, or Book of Changes, is well known as a Chinese divinatory system, but it is more than that. It is one of the oldest texts in existence, and is an ancient and profound Chinese classic. Its approach is in harmony with the Taoist way, and it is one of the earliest attempts by humans to understand the meaning of life and the link between humanity and the Cosmos.

The concepts of the I Ching can be hard to grasp for the modern Western mind. Chinese philosophy, and the I Ching itself, do not contain the belief that evil can ever be eradicated, or even that it should be. Darkness and light, Yin and Yang go hand in hand. When any quality reaches its extreme – joy, sorrow, loss, gain – it tips over into its opposite. The only constant is change.

The I Ching is usually linked with the philosopher Confucius (K'ung Fu-tzu), who promoted the concept of the superior man – a wise and benevolent leader. In his system, individuals deferred to the common good and each person had their rightful place, depending upon experience. Scholars do not agree as to whether or not Confucius wrote many of the judgements/interpretations in the I Ching. However, the I Ching may also be seen as having its roots in ancient ancestor worship, animism and a shamanic culture.

THE MYTH OF THE DISCOVERY OF THE I CHING

The story of the I Ching goes back to one of the Three August Ones, the Emperor Fu Hsi, who was part animal, part shaman and part historical figure. In one version Fu Hsi, ruler of the manifest world, looked up and saw the I Ching symbols dangling from the Heavens. He then looked down and saw similar patterns on the earth. He cast his divine eyes on the markings on birds and animals, and the shapes of their dwellings. He drew on his knowledge and experience of his body, looking close beside him and into the far distance.

Spontaneously he brought forth the Eight Symbols, connecting with the bright spirits and bringing order to the nature of the myriad things in existence. Thus Fu Hsi was the first to use Change to help humankind.

A second story shows Fu Hsi walking on the shores of the Yellow River. As he watched the rippling waters, a dragon horse broke the waves, bearing wonderful markings. In the way of a sage, Fu Hsi watched it carefully, understanding that all knowledge derived from observation of the natural world. In time he came to understanding, and transcribed the markings as the foundation of the I Ching.

Another story tells simply that the shell of the tortoise and the lines upon it were the inspiration for the I Ching. For divination purposes the shell of a tortoise was heated until it cracked, and the lines that resulted were interpreted. The tortoise is a very important animal in the myths of China (and also other cultures such as Native American). In some versions of the Pangu Creation myth (Chapter 2) a tortoise, or turtle, aids Pangu in his task of separating sea and sky. In other stories the goddess Nuwa or Nugua cuts off the legs of a sea turtle and uses them to prop up the sky.

For the Chinese, as for the Native Americans, the tortoise symbolizes the Cosmos. Its back forms a dome, like the sky, and has markings that look like constellations, while the lower part relates to the earth. On a practical note, tortoise shells carried some of the earliest forms of writing.

All of these stories, and more, show the wisdom of the I Ching to arise from and within the natural world. As with so many shamanic cultures, the material world is a metaphor for spirit, and nature an avenue to the mystical.

HISTORY OF THE I CHING

In its purest form, the I Ching is believed to date back at least 5,000 years. Many centuries after the time of the mythical Fu Hsi, in about 1700 BCE, the wisdom of the trigrams was first recorded. In its more sophisticated form of the hexagrams it was compiled in c.1122 BCE by the wise and compassionate ruler of the Chou province, Lord Wen. He was imprisoned by the evil Shang Emperor and while in captivity he had time to meditate on the trigrams, bringing them together to form the 64 hexagrams. He named each of the hexagrams to form the basis of the I Ching as we know it today, and some say he wrote the judgements that express the fundamental meanings. In time King Wen's son vanquished the arrogant Shang and a new Chou dynasty was established. His grandson took over as sovereign, while his uncle, the Duke of Chou acted as regent. The Duke of Chou put the finishing touches to King Wen's work on the hexagrams. Confucius, many centuries later, in the fifth and sixth centuries bce, added discussion and illumination. Thus the I Ching is the distillation of China's most time-honoured wisdom and respected sages. It was essential reading for anyone wishing to be considered educated and cultured in Chinese society.

THE SYMBOLISM OF THE I CHING

The I Ching is a divinatory system that has similarities with runes, ogham and Tarot. However, it is far more primitive than Tarot in that it uses broken and unbroken lines to convey meaning, rather than complex pictures, and it is more basic than the markings of rune stones, because the I Ching is based simply on the interplay of Yin and Yang. However, the interpretations of the I Ching may be extremely subtle and complex, for nothing is static and many things may be possible.

The I Ching is composed of lines, which are either broken or continuous. These are combined in sets of three, and these sets are called *trigrams*. In the most complex system of the I Ching, the eight basic trigrams can be paired into 64 *hexagrams*. Continuous lines are *Yang*, broken lines are *Yin*. The combination of Yin and Yang is what gives the trigram its meaning. The eight trigrams occur in four natural pairs, which balance and complement each other. These appear on the Ba Gua (see Chapter 4).

The trigrams were divined by the Chinese through the drawing of yarrow stalks or the tossing of coins. In all its forms, the I Ching can aid your intuition and enable you to tune in to the changing patterns of the Universe. Like all divinatory systems, it is not the method itself that is important but the way it can stimulate your instincts and open the pathways to the subconscious mind.

USING THE I CHING

As a first step to attuning to the interplay and fluctuations of Yin and Yang, it is possible to access the I Ching through making simple cards. All that is necessary are eight rectangles of card, roughly the size of playing cards. Make sure these are as well-shaped and even as possible, so that handling them is comfortable. On one side draw one of the trigrams. The other side can be left blank or decorated in whatever way seems suitable – however, all the decorations must be identical so the cards cannot be identified from the wrong side.

Once made, tradition states that the cards must be treated with respect by being kept carefully wrapped and handled gently. This is important for opening the mind to this venerable system.

THE TRIGRAMS

The first pair consists of Heaven and Earth, Yang and Yin, being the source of life.

≡ CHI'EN – HEAVEN, SKY
Achievement.

Creativity, logic, courage, focused energy, identity, assertiveness, success, confidence.

Body: head, mind, skull.

Animal: horse, tiger.

Social correspondences: father, sage, commander, elderly men.

Other associations: north-west, white, gold, chrysanthemums, fruit trees, outer garments, cold and ice.

☷ K'UN – EARTH
Acceptance.

Receptivity, consideration intuition, patience, docility, nurturing.

Body: stomach, abdomen, womb.

Animal: ox, cow, mare, ant.

Social correspondences: mother, wise woman, old woman, the general populace.

Other associations: south-west, early autumn, black/dark brown, potatoes, bulbs, tree trunks, seamless cloak that covers all, an old cart carrying everything.

The second pair refers to diffused energy, being Fire and Water (or The Abyss)

▆▆ *LI* – FIRE
Inspiration.

Illumination, cleansing, clarity, communication, clinging to that which feeds.

Body: eye, blood, speech, heart.

Animal: pheasant, turtle, goldfish.

Social correspondences: middle daughter, artists, young women, benefactors, craftsmen.

Other associations: the sun, lightning, shells, armour, south, summer, orange, tomatoes, red and yellow peppers, dry trees and hollows.

▆▆ *K'AN* – WATER, THE ABYSS
Feeling.

Tuning in to emotions, going with the flow, desire, emotion, fearlessness, danger, hardship.

Body: ear, kidney.

Animal: pig, rat, wild boar, bat.

Social correspondences: second son, young men, the sick, trouble-makers, fisherman.

Other associations: wells, moon, rain, rivers, floods, north, winter, blue, reeds, water lilies, willow, alder.

The third pairing refers to movement.

▆▆ *CHEN* – THUNDER
Regeneration.

Seeds of new life, arousal, surprise, spontaneity, male sexuality.

Body: voice, foot.

Animal: dragon, eagle.

Social correspondences: eldest son, men below middle age, prince, inventor, musician.

Other associations: thunderstorms, hurricanes, volcanoes, east, spring, yellow, flowers, evergreens, bamboo.

▤ *SUN* – WIND/WOOD
Persistence.

Gentle but determined, progress, adaptability, flexibility, endurance, justice.

Body: thigh, legs, lungs, nerves.

Animal: cockerel, snake, tiger.

Social correspondences: women below middle age, teachers, travellers, business people.

Other associations: fragrances, clouds, ropes, webs, south-east, early summer, green, grass, poppies, tall trees.

The fourth pairing refers to stillness.

▤ *KEN* – MOUNTAIN
Vision.

Stillness, withdrawal, silence meditation, spirituality.

Body: hand, back.

Animal: dog, bull, leopard, mouse.

Social correspondence: youngest son, boys, prisoners, worshippers, monks.

Other associations: opening door, narrow path, walls, watchtowers, north-east, early spring, purple, mountain plants, nut trees.

▤ *TUI* – LAKE
Secrecy.

Dreams, psychic, magic, pleasure, joy, tranquillity, healing.

Body: mouth, smiling lips.

Animal: sheep, deer.

Social correspondences: youngest daughter, girls, concubines, sorceresses.

Other associations: valleys, mist, harvest, west, autumn, red, magnolia, gardenia, spices, bleached trees

EXAMPLES FOR INTERPRETATION

The eight trigrams will give you a message that is simple, but profound. Think of a question and draw a card for your answer.

Example 1

Should I apply for a certain job? Drawing *Chi'en* would give you a fairly clear 'yes' to using your confidence, but would *K'un* mean you should stay where you are? Or does it mean using your intuition in your approach?

Example 2

Is my new relationship right for me? *Tui* would seem to say 'yes' – but is there a hidden side? *Chen* could mean it takes you out of your comfort zone but spells excitement.

These are very simplified examples that hardly do justice to the subtle and sophisticated tradition that has been studied by philosophers for millennia. However, as an aid to the intuition you have the choice to return to the message of Fu Hsi and see what your inner journey reveals as you work with the trigrams.

Further reading

Larousse Encyclopaedia of Mythology (Batchworth, 1959)

Birrell, Anee, *Chinese Myths* (British Museum Press, 2000)

Birrell, Anee (trans.), *The Classic of the Mountains and Seas* (Penguin, 1999)

Blofield, John, *I Ching, the Book of Change* (Unwin Mandala, 1984)

Ch'eng-En, Wu, *Monkey* (Penguin, 1973)

Craze, Richard, *Feng Shui – A Beginner's Guide, and Feng Shui – A Complete Guide* (Hodder & Stoughton Educational, 1996)

Duane, O.B. & Hutchinson, N., *Chinese Myths and Legends* (Brockhampton, 1998)

Palmer, Martin, *Elements of Taoism* (Element, 1991)

Palmer, Martin & Xiaomin, Zhao, *Essential Chinese Mythology* (Thorsons, 1997)

Rawson, Philip & Legeza, Laszlo, *Tao, the Chinese Philosophy of Time and Change* (Thames & Hudson, 1995)

Tzu, Lao, *Tao Te Ching* (Penguin, 1972)

Walters, Derek, *Chinese Mythology* (Aquarian, 1992)

Whittaker, Clio (ed.), *Oriental Mythology* (Grange Books, 1989)

Index